Career Perspective:
Your Choice of Work

Celia Denues

San Jose City College

Charles A. Jones Publishing Company
Worthington, Ohio

To Caroline, Bill, and Charlie

....

   In our particular society, work organization looms
so large as a separate and specialized system of
things, and work experience is so fateful a part of
every man's life, that we cannot make much head-
way as students of society and of social psychology
without using work as one of our main laboratories.

Everett C. Hughes

....

From *American Journal of Sociology*, vol. 57, no. 5 (March,
1952). Reprinted with permission of University of Chicago
Press.

1 2 3 4 5 6 7 8 9 10 / 76 75 74 73 72

Library of Congress Catalog Card Number: 72-181375
International Standard Book Number: 0-8396-0008-9

Printed in the United States of America

Preface

The purpose of this book is to assist the individual who wishes to find his place in the world of work. The rapid and inevitable changes that are taking place within the world make great demands on the individual who must face the unique opportunities for work.

The underlying principles of *Career Perspective: Your Choice of Work* are:

• There is a process for choosing one's work which can be trusted. It is based on experiencing, assessing experience, evaluating and drawing conclusions and then projecting new experiences, assessing them, evaluating, etc. We believe that, for the student, the experience of the classroom and counseling programs can enable him to know more clearly the experiences he wishes to project and actualize and how to proceed to accumulate them.

• Choosing one's work is more than merely acquiring a job or considering selection of an occupation; it is choosing a way of life and, for this reason, the choice must be appropriate and fulfilling for each individual.

• One's career path is not a decision but a developmental process; the choice of work must be made again and again.

Career Perspective is a guide to the process of self-analysis and evaluation, a direction for the task of scrutinizing the world of work and a set of clues for making career decisions. It may be used effectively as a springboard for pertinent discussions by the readers based on their varying concepts of what is true, encouraging them through honest dialogue to accept more freely their own uniqueness and to assess more genuinely the real world. Much of the material grew out of student discussion and sometimes may reflect dialogue that took place in the classroom.

In preparation of the manuscript I am indebted to the scholars whose research and writing have formed the basis for understanding the nature of work choice. To my students I owe an increased awareness of the relationship between theory and application that developed with frank discussions of their expanding experiences.

Many of these experiences are included as case studies in the book.

Most helpful in reading and criticizing the material were Dr. Calvin Cotrell, Dr. Myron Hamer, Dr. Herb Brum, Dr. Henry Shocksnider, Dr. Dean Hauenstein, and Dr. Calvin Stewart. In developing the manuscript Dr. June Grant Shane offered significant suggestions and in the final reading Dr. Mary-Margaret Scobey made an invaluable contribution.

For her faithful, expert assistance in typing I am grateful to Emily Stewart who made this manuscript possible. I would like also to express my appreciation to the artists, writers, and speakers who graciously permitted use of their works to complement with distinction the theme of this book.

Celia Denues

Contents

Introduction: The Choice Before You

How important to you is your choice of a career? Whatever your answer may be, do not underestimate the importance of a significant choice. Your first response may be that your career will determine how much money you make, but your choice of career will determine much more than this. It will determine your life style, your friends, and your enjoyment of life.

Life style refers to a manner of living: indoors or outdoors, with people or by oneself, with ideas or with things, working early or late, under pressure or without pressure, with routine or with varying activities. Only you know the style of living that best suits you.

Approximately one-half of your waking hours will be spent in employment. Such an investment in time and energy must be considered as living your life; and spending your life forces in a satisfying and challenging career that you have chosen is one way to ensure yourself of joy in living.

The persons you work with become an important part of your personal relationships. People who retire appear to miss these relationships more than the work itself, which points up the wisdom of working with people you truly respect and admire.

1

What criteria should you use to choose a career?   Of yourself, you must ask: "What do I like to do? What do I do well? What do I think is worth doing?" About the world of work you must ask: "What work is available? Is the education or training for this work available to me?"

What are the obstacles to your making a wise choice?
You may have already realized that one of your chief obstacles is outside pressure: pressure from parents, pressure from friends, even pressure from other people who suggest "good" careers to follow.

But you may be solely responsible for other obstacles. One of these may be your unwillingness to face the facts. Sooner or later, in order to choose wisely, you must accept yourself: your talents, your limitations, your mental capacity, your physical strength. You must stop striving for the impossible or for an inappropriate career.

Another obstacle may be the slow development of mature values. A choice of a career made now because of its status in the community may prove disappointing ten years from now. A choice made now because of the money to be earned may leave you feeling cheated in later years. A knowledge of your own value system is the only reliable basis for selecting a career.

How can one's interests, aptitudes, and values be determined?
The most familiar method of determining interests and aptitudes is by taking tests. Fortunately, tests today are better than ever because more and more research is used to compile test data.

In addition to tests, it is valuable to accumulate work experience such as summer jobs, part time jobs, and volunteer work. Your work experience, past and present, reveals what is acceptable and satisfying to you. Academic subjects and specific courses may also demonstrate your competence in certain areas and help you compare yourself with other students.

Another method of determining the direction you should take is researching careers that seem to appeal to you. Reading up-to-date, reliable information published by authorities in the field and interviewing personnel people, career persons and, most important of all, individuals who are employed in the work you are considering will supply helpful information. When possible, you should visit institutions or places of work connected with the career.

Learning about your aptitudes, competences, and the demands of work must be followed by *careful assessment of your true and natural self.* This book is planned to help you answer the questions necessary to make your own significant choice of work.

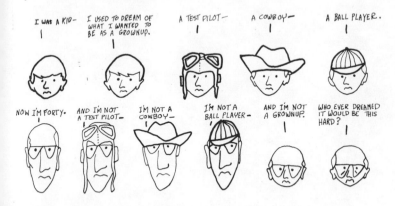

FEIFFER'S FABLES .....

I WAS A KID—   I USED TO DREAM OF WHAT I WANTED TO BE AS A GROWNUP.   A TEST PILOT—   A COWBOY—   A BALL PLAYER.

NOW I'M FORTY.   AND I'M NOT A TEST PILOT—   I'M NOT A COWBOY—   I'M NOT A BALL PLAYER—   AND I'M NOT A GROWNUP.   WHO EVER DREAMED IT WOULD BE THIS HARD?

Part I
The World of Work

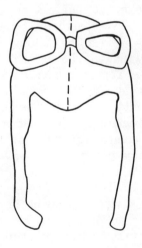

1

Why Work?

If you were rich enough to do anything you wanted all through the day, through the weeks, months, and years, what would you do?

"I would lie on the beach and gaze at the follicles on my legs," said one student.

"Just lie there all day long and gaze at your legs?"

"Well, after a while I would take a walk up and down the beach."

"You mean you would spend your days lying on the beach, looking at your legs, or walking up and down the beach?"

"Well, actually, I would gather shells and make jewelry."

And so the budding artist committed himself to an activity that could be labeled "work."

You may have answered, "I would travel." Again, we would ask, "You would travel throughout your lifetime? You would give up the roots of home and community? You would associate, for the most part, with those who speak a different language, eat different food, cherish a different culture?" Some persons might be suited to this life. For some it would be a lonesome, shallow life.

What do you really enjoy doing? Is it tutoring children, skydiving, or playing in a rock group? Does your preference run to "drags," the Experimental College, encounter groups, or taking part in relevant politics?

You may enjoy many kinds of activities and there may be more you would enjoy if you knew about them. For example,

Bertrand Russell, orphaned at fourteen, found a joy in living through his study of the principles of higher mathematics. Some experiences, of course, you will like more than others; some you will enjoy for only a short time. Knowing what you enjoy most, however, is crucial to knowing how you will want to spend most of your time and energy throughout your lifetime.

Just as "the proper study of mankind is man" so the proper study of work is activity. If you ask, "Why work?" you could answer, "Why do anything?" Work at its best is the activity you have chosen as a means of fulfilling yourself; it is "your thing." It is your way of relating to life and to others, as well as a way of supporting yourself.

Yet it cannot be denied that many persons look upon work as a curse and dread every working day. Think of the people you know who hate to go to work. Most people who dislike their work may be bored. They may lack opportunity for self-expression and for advancement. Or they don't like their co-workers or their working conditions. They may be given little responsibility and routine jobs. "No challenge," said one student, "an eighth grader could do my job."

Do you know what you most dislike about work? It is important to answer this question because then you must ask yourself, "Is it work I dislike, or is it this kind of work I dislike?" In your judgment, are undesirable qualities inherent in work, or of only certain kinds of work, or of a certain place of work? Can these evils be avoided or minimized? It is our experience that they can and *must* be avoided.

What, specifically, are the good things about work? You might answer, "What would the world be like if no one worked?" For like love, work makes the world go round. Our civilization and standard of living are dependent upon a working society. This is the crux of the matter.

Purposeful Living

Work gives a man purpose in living. It gets him up in the morning and out in the world of action and aliveness. It gives structure to his days, weeks, months, years. Like Pippa, he can really enjoy a vacation. He realizes that certain hours of his days are productive and that he is of use in the world while he stretches his muscles and brain to keep them active and fit. He does not need to be one of *A Thousand Clowns* because he believes in the work that is his.

Earning One's Way

A very real benefit of working is earning money. Without it man is limited in the goods and experiences that he may have; with it he realizes independence because he can take advantage of many kinds of opportunities. In addition, he feels a sense of self-esteem when he realizes that someone is willing to pay him money for what he does.

Relatedness

The persons with whom a man works become well known and appreciated; some become friends. The cooperation needed on the job results in loyalty and sympathy that enlarges human understanding and affection. Coffee breaks, lunch hours, recreation clubs expand into testimonial dinners, gifts and remembrances, and actions of personal concern.

What happens to the individuals you know who have retired? Are they not continually looking for someone to talk to and to listen to or to be near? They may have returned to work wishing to enjoy again the comraderie and fellowship of a congenial working group.

Personal Development

The simplest job requires that we learn to follow directions and to get along with at least one other person. More complex work requires greater concentration, adjustment to more people, and some ability to innovate. Most work demands an expression of talents, aptitudes, thoughts, and feelings. Work can stimulate development of the best in us. Sometimes work that does not demand an expression of our innate abilities may seem tedious.

....

Wanda's Second Choice.   Wanda Parrish tested superior on her college entrance exams. Her grades in school were almost all A's. Instead of a four-year college program she chose a two-year course in cosmetology because, she said, "I plan to marry soon." A counselor questioned her choice and her long-term goals, but Wanda held steadfast to her purpose.

Three years later, Wanda appeared abruptly at the counselor's door. "Please help me," she pleaded. "I know the admission date is past but I must get back to school. I am unhappy and bored with my life. My husband said emphatically last night, 'Why don't you go back to college and try something else?' "

Together Wanda and the counselor planned that she enroll in some experimental courses, and through a special arrangement with the administration, she was permitted a limited course load.

"During the next semester, Wanda took various tests to guide her self-understanding and she also explored her interests through her course work. At one point she decided to be a psychiatrist, "because for one thing, I do well working with parents and their families in the PTA." But when she considered that she was thirty years of age and that she had growing children, the long training necessary for a career in psychiatry seemed unrealistic.

After two years, Wanda was graduated with honors from her local junior college. Now, in a nearby state college, she is continuing studies to become a high school counselor.

....

Work and Happiness

Carl Jung said, "The supreme goal of man is to fulfill himself as a creative, unique individual, according to his own innate potentialities and within the limits of reality."

Because work, more than anything else, can be a way of life that is challenging, enriching, and fulfilling, it appears almost reckless to give little thought and preparation for choosing wisely. Like pollution, cancer, and overpopulation, neglected at the peril of mankind, careless career choice can stifle the individual's joy of living.

Self-fulfillment is so cherished in our land that we consider the pursuit of happiness an inalienable right.

For Exploration and Discussion

1. During the class hour, exchange occupational experiences with other members of the class.

2. During the week observe and evaluate some workers on the basis of their enjoyment or satisfaction. When appropriate or possible, discuss their choice of work with them.

3. Based on the theory that work has many physical, psychological, social, and economic benefits, discuss in class what happens to persons who are unemployed or underemployed.

4. Without doing extensive research, speculate about the relationship of automation and other technologies to satisfaction and dissatisfaction people find in their work.

5. A psychologist stated that man must work to be fulfilled. He suggests that man must volunteer for unpaid work if paid work is not available. How would society be affected if this occurred? Give examples of unpaid volunteer work.

6. Research the term "the Protestant Ethic."

7. What do we need to know about the nature of work that is now unknown, only surmised? Can such research be instituted or is it now being undertaken?

8. Write a paper for your instructor, to be used later in individual vocational counseling, referring to these items: your tentative vocational choice, if any; your ideal choice if it were possible; your strengths and weaknesses, as far as you know them in academic work and as a person; jobs, of any duration, that you have held up to this time and what you thought of them.

9. Read the chapter on "Work" in *Conquest of Happiness* by Bertrand Russell. (New York: Signet Key Books, 1951)
Read the chapter entitled "Jobs" in *Growing Up, Absurd* by Paul Goodman. (New York: Random House, 1960)
Read the section "Work" in *The Sane Society* by Erich Fromm. (New York: Holt, Rinehart & Winston, 1955)

2

Work Versus Play

Work is activity and, likewise, play is activity. Yet in the minds of most people these two concepts are opposite in meaning.

Clarifying Work and Play

Webster's New Collegiate Dictionary defines *play* as "an exercise or action for amusement or diversion"; it defines *work* as "an exertion of strength or faculties to accomplish something."

One might ask: Can a single activity provide diversion and amusement and also accomplish something? Some persons who might answer yes are professional athletes, highly paid entertainers, wealthy government officials, and successful businessmen.

As parents and psychologists have acquired greater understanding of the way children grow, they have realized that child's play is a serious thing. Consequently, intensive study has been made of educational toys, children's literature, and how and with whom children play. Professional workers in recreation attempt to make children's play contribute to personal and social growth. Lessons for parents have been developed on how to play with children.

"Children's play is the equivalent of man's work," says Elizabeth Gregg, author of *What To Do When There's Nothing To Do*. Her thesis is that the child who does not learn to play is handicapped. In order to put his energies to good use as he grows older, a child must learn to experiment with things. In play he learns to manipulate objects — he learns what he is able to do with things. In play he gains understanding of his world, confidence in himself, and an expansion of his own abilities.

What Gregg has said about child's play is also true of man's work.

Contrasting Work and Play

Since we cannot differentiate between work and play by the seriousness or significance of an activity, how else can we contrast them? We can try to differentiate between work and play by saying that one requires a great deal of energy and the other does not; that one demands cooperation and the other does not. But we realize that these distinctions are not valid. We come nearer the truth when we say that one you receive pay for, the other you do not; one you are compelled to do, the other you are not; one demands skill and training, the other does not. However, even these comparisons will not always be valid.

An authority on play, Johan Huizinga, describes five characteristics of play from his study of play elements in culture.

1. Play is a voluntary activity, never a physical necessity or a moral duty.
2. Play is not ordinary or real life, but this is not to say that play may not be intense or serious ... it is rather an interlude in our daily lives, an end in itself.
3. Play is secluded and limited, containing its own course and meaning; it begins and is over at a specific moment. Yet it can be repeated.

4. Play creates order; in fact, it is order. It is inside a "play-ground"; slight deviations from the rules spoil the game.
5. Last, the play community tends to become permanent after the game is over, for in the course of playing it has become an "in-group" having already shared a common experience. (1)

The first two characteristics listed by Huizinga delineate a genuine difference between work and play, that play as an activity is voluntary and that it is an end in itself. Both work and play have value. Both work and play may be serious; both can be creative, challenging, and social. The one real difference then between them seems to be purpose.

Purpose of Work

Man's purpose in work is to change something or to create or produce something. Man's purpose in play, however, is to relax, exercise, entertain, amuse or refresh himself. We can easily see that the same activity may be work or play, according to the purpose of the doer. Sports, fine art, crafts, and hobbies fall easily into either category. For example, Winston Churchill laid brick and painted in oils for relaxation, Willie Mays plays ball for other men's relaxation and entertainment, and a college professor at Stanford has his backyard occupied by Airedales he raises, trains, and shows for his personal pleasure. Obviously, it is the purpose of the activity that determines its classification as work or play.

Avocation Versus Vocation

The purpose of an activity may change and with it the classification. Avocation may become vocation when unusual success or talent in a hobby leads an individual to make it a career. Actually, winning teams or successful amateur theatrical groups often produce one or two professionals. Further, the superb cook may open a restaurant and the young woman who makes her own clothes may become a designer.

Conversely, an avocation may be too significant to be regarded as a task to be routinely accomplished. The writer, the singer, or the photographer may wish to make his living doing something else and to save for his avocation only his finest and truest expression.

Work and Responsibility

Work as a chosen activity compares with play as a chosen activity. Both are fulfilling in their own way. Each demands energy, attention, acceptance of the nature and demands of the activity, and each requires a commitment in time and interest.

Production is the goal of work but not of play. At any moment play may be discontinued, but work must continue until the task is done. The beginnings of maturity are reflected in willingness to accept this responsibility.

Work and Belonging

Like play, work is a way of relating to life, to the world, to nature, and to others. Erich Fromm says that man has only two ways of relating to life constructively: one is by love and the other by productive activity. The very act of accomplishing a day of work permits man to feel at one with the purposes of the world and to feel a needed part of society. Failure to sense this oneness results in disquieting alienation. In Arthur Miller's *Death of a Salesman* Biff understands this when he says to his father, "Dad, I can't take hold — I don't know why it is, but I can't take hold."

Frustration

Having lost a sense of oneness with life, or never having gained it, some persons despair of finding any activity for which they are willing to live.(2) In work they see only fragmentation, boredom, and wasted energy, with no meaning, enjoyment, or fulfillment.

Admittedly, too many jobs fail to challenge the heart, imagination, or spirit. This is a problem. It may be that with the help of the new technology man can devise ways to free himself from the mundane and free his spirit to perform willingly, if not eagerly.

For some, no jobs are available. For the unemployed, a hollow despair is echoed in a selection from *Hamlet's* gravediggers' scene employed in *Hair*, the rock musical of youth and frustration.

> I have of late
> But wherefore I know not
> Lost all my mirth.
> This goodly frame, the earth
> Seems to me a sterile promontory
> This most excellent canopy, the air
> Look you,
> This brave o'erhanging firmament
> This majestical roof fretted with golden fire,
> Why, it appears no other thing to me
> Than a foul and pestilent congregation of vapor. (3)

Mastery

Play is mastery for the child; for the young adult, work is mastery. To understand materials and to shape and command them is to test the environment and oneself. The child precariously perches one block on top of another, the school athlete leaps over the hurdles and races toward the finish, the housewife plans a nutritious meal, and the mayor plots the city's course. The steady accumulation of mastery over many tasks accounts for the developing and expanding personality until that human goal is reached — to fulfill one's potentiality.

Spontaneity

One of the characteristics of the child at play is his spontaneity. "But," Jean Piaget asks, "are not the investigations of the child and those of pure science equally spontaneous?" "For," he continues, "science and art are superior games and can only be differentiated from just games because their spontaneity is in a measure controlled by reality." (4) While most work must be adapted to reality, a natural, free response to the immediate task is characteristic of the productive, creative moment.

It is possible to pursue with delight many facets of work and play activities. Letting your imagination explore the possibilities, you can develop your own criteria of differentiation and relationship, and your sense of initative and enthusiasm for the activities before you.

Mark Twain made the classic statement on work versus play in his *Adventures of Tom Sawyer*:

Tom appeared on the sidewalk with a bucket of whitewash and a long-handled brush. He surveyed the fence, and all the gladness left him and a deep melancholy settled down on his spirit. Thirty yards of board fence nine feet high. Life to him seemed hollow, and existence but a burden. Sighing he dipped his brush and passed it along the topmost plank; repeated the operation; did it again; compared the insignificant whitewashed streak with the far-reaching continent of unwhitewashed fence, and sat down on a tree-box discouraged.

Tom began to think of the fun he had planned for this day, and his sorrows multiplied. Soon the free boys would come tripping along on all sorts of delicious expeditions, and they would make a world of fun of him for having to work—and the very thought of it burnt him like fire. At this dark and hopeless moment an inspiration burst upon him! Nothing less than a great, magnificent inspiration.

He took up his brush and went tranquilly to work. Ben Rogers hove in sight presently — the very boy of all boys whose ridicule he had been dreading.

Tom went on whitewashing—paid no attention to Ben staring at him and eating an apple. Ben stared a moment and then said:

"Hi-ya! You're up a stump, ain't you!"

No answer. Tom surveyed his last touch with the eye of an artist, then he gave his brush another gentle sweep and surveyed the result, as before. Ben ranged up alongside of him. Tom's mouth watered for the apple, but he stuck to his work. Ben said:

"Hello, old chap, you got to work, hey?"

Tom wheeled suddenly and said:

"Why, it's you, Ben! I warn't noticing."

"Say, I'm goin' a-swimming, I am. Don't you wish you could? But, of course, you'd druther work, wouldn't you? Course you would!"

Tom contemplated the boy a bit and said:

"What do you call work?"

"Why, ain't that work?"

Tom resumed his whitewashing and answered carelessly:

"Well, maybe it is, and maybe it ain't. All I know is, it suits Tom Sawyer."

"Oh, come now, you don't mean to let on that you like it?"

The brush continued to move.

"Like it? Well, I don't see why I oughtn't to like it. Does a boy get a chance to whitewash a fence every day?"

That put the thing in a new light. Ben stopped nibbling his apple. Tom swept his brush daintily back and forth — stepped back to note the effect — added a touch here and there—criticized the effect again—Ben watching every move and getting more and more absorbed. Presently he said:

"Say, Tom, let me whitewash a little."

Tom considered, was about to consent, but he altered his mind:

"No—no—I reckon it wouldn't hardly do, Ben. You see Aunt Polly's awful particular about this fence — right here on the street, you know—but if it was the back fence I wouldn't mind and she wouldn't. Yes, she's awful particular about this fence; it's got to be done very careful; I reckon there ain't a boy in a thousand, maybe two thousand, that can do it the way it's got to be done."

"No—is that so? Oh, come, now—lemme just try. Only just a little—I'd let you, if you was me, Tom."

"Ben, I'd like to, honest injun; but Aunt Polly — well, Jim wanted to do it, but she wouldn't let him. Now, don't you see how I'm fixed? If you was to tackle this fence and anything was to happen to it—"

"Oh, shucks, I'll be just as careful. Now lemme try. Say —I'll give you the core of my apple."

"Well, here — No, Ben, now don't. I'm afeard—"

"I'll give you all of it!"

Tom gave up the brush with reluctance in his face, but joy in his heart. And while Ben worked and sweated in the sun, the retired artist sat on a barrel in the shade close by, dangled his legs, munched his apple, and planned the slaughter of more innocents. There was no lack of material: boys happened along every little while; they came to jeer, but remained to whitewash.

Tom had a nice, good, idle time all the while, plenty of company — and the fence had three coats of whitewash on it.

Tom said to himself that it was not such a hollow world after all. He had discovered a great law of human action, without knowing it; as he barely comprehended that Work consists of whatever a body is obliged to do, and that Play consists of whatever a body is not obliged to do. (5)

Play and Civilization

Perhaps the most profound statement about the nature of play has been made by Huizinga, who says:

> ... civilization is rooted in noble play and if it is to unfold in full dignity and style, it cannot afford to neglect the play element. ... real civilization cannot exist in the absence of a certain play element, for civilization pre-supposes limitation and mastery of the self, the ability not to confuse its own tendencies with the ultimate and highest goal, but to understand that it is enclosed within certain bounds fully accepted. (6)

Another argument is that all human action is play. No less an authority than Plato expressed his belief in this matter.

> Now human affairs are hardly worth considering in earnest, and yet we must be in earnest about them. . . . I say that about serious matters a man should be serious, and about a matter which is not serious he should not be serious; and that God is the natural and worthy object of our most serious and blessed endeavors, for man is made to be the plaything of God, and this, truly considered, is the best (part) of him; wherefore, also every man and woman should work seriously, and pass life in the noblest of pastimes. At present they think that their serious pursuits should be for the sake of their sports, for they deem war a serious pursuit which must be managed well for the sake of peace; but the truth is that there neither is, nor has been, nor ever will be, either amusement or instruction in any degree worth speaking of in war, which is nevertheless deemed by us to be the most serious of our pursuits. And, therefore, as we say, every one of us should live the life of peace as long and as well as he can. And what is the right way of living? Are we to live in sports always? If so, what kind of sports? We ought to live sacrificing, and singing, and dancing, and then a man will be able to propitiate the Gods, and to defend himself against his enemies. . ." (7)

For Exploration and Discussion

1. Categorize workers you observe on television, in sports, recreation, and in leisure activity who appear to enjoy working.

2. Discuss with friends or acquaintances who are anti-establishment their concepts of work and play.

3. What is the message that groups of non-conforming young people are presenting to the world? Are they alienated? Uncommitted? Courageous?

4. Interview persons who have been in the Peace Corps or Vista to find out their reactions to their work in these groups.

5. What leisure time activities are meaningful to man? Differentiate idleness and leisure activity.

6. What should be the role of flexibility and creativity in both work and play?

7. If a guaranteed annual income is made available to all, what could be its effect on workers? Read arguments for and against this proposal.

8. In our society, who are the victors and who the victims of the structure of work?

References

1. Johan Huizinga, *Homeo Ludens*: "A Study of the Play Element in Culture" as quoted in Max Kaplan, *Leisure in America* (New York: John Wiley & Sons Inc., 1960), pp. 20-21. Reprinted with permission from the publisher.
2. Robert J. Havighurst, "Youth in Exploration and Man Emergent," in Henry Borow, ed., *Man in a World of Work* (Boston: Houghton-Mifflin Company, 1964), p. 231.
3. William Shakespeare, *Hamlet* Act II, scene 2.
4. Jean Piaget, "Criterion of Play." Eric Larrabee and Rolf Meyersohn, eds., *Mass Leisure* (Glencoe, Ill.: Free Press, 1958), pp. 69-70.
5. Mark Twain, *Adventures of Tom Sawyer* (New York: Harper & Brothers, 1875), pp. 12-18.
6. Johan Huizinga, "The Play Element in Contemporary Civilization," Eric Larrabee and Rolf Meyersohn, eds., *Mass Leisure* (Glencoe, Ill.: Free Press, 1958), pp. 83, 84.
7. Benjamin Jowett, trans. *The Dialogues of Plato* (New York: Random House, 1937), II, 558-559.

3

Choosing the Possible

"I would do well in school," remarked one student, "if it weren't for reality." In the world of work you must come smack up against reality!

Job Limitations

To choose your work you must consider what is possible for you with your abilities and your opportunities. You must also include the opportunities for your education, training, and placement. Another limitation to your choice is what is needed in the working world, a factor considered more carefully in the next chapter. Here we shall consider restrictions related to your personal situation rather than to the culture in which you live.

The meaning of limitations varies with individuals. For some, limitations arise when reaching a goal is difficult. For others, "difficult" is not to be confused with "impossible"; the difficult takes more time, but can be realized with the proper amount of effort. When assessing difficulties you should not overlook the strength of your own desire for a certain goal nor your ability to persevere in attaining that goal.

Job Expectations

What have you a right to expect from your lifetime of work? How much can you expect of a job? Perfection? Do you have a perfect marriage? Do you expect to have a perfect marriage? Do you know anyone who has a perfect marriage? How good is good? When is a job acceptable? When good? When excellent? When superlative? When is a job unendurable? When endurable?

A set of standards can serve as a guide as you develop your career. For each of you the criteria will be different, according to your individual sensibilities.

One group of students listed the following traits to characterize the *unendurable*:

Unendurable:

1. Poor pay

2. Unreasonable employer

3. Unpleasant working conditions

4. Suspicious co-workers

5. Long or irregular hours

6. Distasteful work

A job in a cannery might be endurable for a summer because of relatively good pay, but unendurable for a longer time. One student, working throughout the summer to enable her to continue college in the fall, contrived games as she dropped one cherry after another into successive cans of fruit. Modifying a few traits in the unendurable category might make a job endurable, for example, changing poor pay to good pay or suspicious co-workers to congenial co-workers.

The students characterized a *superlative* job in this manner:

Superlative:

1. Excellent salary

2. Enjoyable activity

3. Just, understanding employer

4. Pleasant environment

5. Stimulating co-workers

6. Challenging work

7. Reasonable working hours

Deleting a few traits characterizing the superlative job might result in its being excellent or merely good, but on the whole satisfactory. Since each person is unique, the importance of each trait varies according to the value he places upon it. What is unendurable to you might be quite agreeable to another.

For what would you settle? Surely for nothing less than good. Try for excellent. With luck and good fortune you might be one of the few to have a superlative career. You will probably start at a lesser level of expectation and work toward greater satisfaction and career development.

Personal Investment

To some people, a job is a job, is a job, a good and pleasant way to earn a living. To others, a job is a vocation, a "calling," a dedication to the welfare of mankind and his environment.

In a study conducted by Robert Havighurst at the University of Chicago, people of different ages working in many occupations reported their feelings about satisfaction from their work. It developed that the workers could be divided into two groups. Group A liked the challenge of their jobs, felt creative in their work, and with much satisfaction sensed that their work merited respect and was of service to people. Those in Group B liked the people they worked with, and in the activity of work found a pleasant routine. Both groups, moreover, liked to earn money, and from it gained a sense of self-respect. The author concluded that work has a different meaning for different people; that work may be either "ego-involving" or "society-maintaining." (1)

In ego-involving work, the individual lives for his job. His life is organized around it and, indeed, would be empty without it. He takes his work home with him and on vacation carries it along. For him it has priority number one. Such ego-involving jobs, free from automation and mass production and controlled by the worker as to when and how he should work, fall into these categories: executive positions in business and government, research work, dramatics, writing, college teaching, religious vocations, medicine, law, small business ownership, ownership of a one-family farm, and in some cases cabinet making and other skilled crafts.

Society-maintaining work has a much less important place in a person's life than does the ego-involving type. While a society-maintaining job may satisfy a person's ego and help him achieve an identity, it is not the central organizing force for him that an ego-involving occupation is for another person. Occupations of this type are generally paid by the hour for a fixed number of hours. Although the work may require a great deal of skill, it seldom demands prolonged attention that leads a man to worry about it when he is not actually working. Some examples are: factory operations, clerical jobs, retail sales work, some technical jobs, many service jobs, almost all unskilled and some skilled labor, many jobs in transportation and communications, and many jobs in the skilled trades. The satisfactions derived from this kind of work are likely to be those of association with friends on the job, the money earned, and a pleasant or at least tolerable routine for passing the time.

We could add that for one person a particular job would be ego-involving and for another that same job could be society-maintaining. One person might also treat a job in an ego-involved way and another would treat the same job as society-maintaining. An instance here could easily be school teaching, police work, or selling.

Job Satisfaction

You might like to compare your ideas about job satisfaction with those expressed by various workers.

One research study was conducted among 200 engineers and accountants. The workers were asked in one interview what experiences at work had a marked effect in increasing their job satisfaction. Second interviews were conducted to ask the workers what experiences had resulted in job dissatisfaction.

Five factors stood out as strong determinants of job satisfaction: achievement, recognition of achievement, work itself, responsibility, and advancement. A completely different set of factors caused job dissatisfaction: company policy and administration, supervision, salary, interpersonal relations and working conditions. A good environment prevented job dissatisfaction but did not create true job happiness. True job happiness came from the nature of the work itself. (2)

Another study of workers in various types of jobs attempted to find the amount of satisfaction in work. Three questions were asked:

1. If you could start over, would you go into the same kind of work again, or what would you like to do?

2. Suppose you could get the same pay no matter what kind of work you did, of all the kinds of work you can think of, what would you like to do best?

3. How would you feel about a son of yours going into your kind of work?

The worker was classified as satisfied if he gave the following combination of answers:

1. He would go into the same kind of work again, if he could start over.

2. He would like best the same kind of work he was now doing at the same pay.

3. He approves of having a son go into his kind of work or says a son should do as he likes.

Any other combination of answers placed a person in the dissatisfied category. The result was dissatisfaction from 69 per cent of the workers. (3)

Your Commitment

You may not know at this time how much of your energy you wish to put into a job. Perhaps you do not know yourself well enough to understand what is possible or preferable for you. However, you can make a commitment to live fully, to be involved with life, to develop your interests, your talents, your friends and be a part of your generation. Only the future can reveal whether your fulfillment will come in large part from your work or mainly from other activities.

Whichever eventuality occurs, do not accept deadening, useless work. A woman who knew how to live sounded a warning:

> "You'll be old and you never lived, and you kind of feel silly to lie down and die and never have lived, to have been a job chaser and never have lived." (4)

For Exploration and Discussion

1. If, as Thoreau said, men "live lives of quiet desperation," what does he imply of their working hours?

2. Support your position on Emerson's statement, "Things are in the saddle and ride mankind."

3. What relation is there between work experience, motivation, and morale? Examine your own experiences as a basis for your opinion.

4. Write a job description for a job you hold or have held recently, in which you improved the nature of the work in a real and possible way.

5. Recent research on why employees are quitting their jobs in large numbers resulted in a social psychologist's report that workers are now demanding meaningful work with responsibility. His interest in the relationship between job enrichment and work motivation prompted him to write a book, *Motivation Through the Work Itself* (New York: American Management Association, 1969). The author, Robert Ford, also has written an article, "The Obstinate Employee" in *Psychology Today*, November, 1969, pp. 33-35. Read this for a new positive approach to the nature of work.

6. Harvey Swados wrote, "It is one thing to endure stupid, mindless, endless, maddeningly monotonous work if you are an immigrant desperately eager to get a toehold in a new world. . . . it is quite another to face a lifetime of work in which you cannot possibly take any pride and the only reason you stay there is that the salesman, the brassy voice of America, has conned you into overbuying . . ."
Defend or reject this statement.

7. Read from the writings of economists John Kenneth Galbraith, Robert Heilbroner, or Robert Theobold about the ways our economic system might be restructured to make production and distribution of products more satisfactory.

References

1. Robert Havighurst, "Youth in Exploration and Man Emergent," in Henry Borow, ed., *Man in a World at Work* (Boston: Houghton-Mifflin Company, 1964), pp. 225ff.

2. Frederick Herzberg, "Motivation, Morale, and Money." *Psychology Today*, March 1968, p. 45.

3. Elizabeth Lyman, "Occupational Difference in the Value Attached to Work" in Herman J. Peters and James C. Hansen, eds., *Vocational Guidance and Career Development* (New York: Macmillan Company, 1966), pp. 22-24.

4. Gertrude Stein, *Brewsie and Willie*, (New York: Random House, 1946), p. 108.

4

The Changing World

As he stepped down the narrow earth ladder onto the unknown surface of the moon, Neil Armstrong made the prophetic statement, "One short step for man, one giant leap for mankind." With that act, science fiction came alive. This momentous achievement, a gift from this generation to succeeding generations, epitomizes the drastic change taking place in the world that is your heritage. It represents all the sophistication of invention, automation, social planning, and communication that is the result of man's ingenuity. It means rapid and dramatic changes in employment. To survive and succeed as a worker in this sky-rocketing society is a very real challenge to you who are entering the labor force. Fortunately, synchronized planning and cooperative procedures are an acknowledged necessity in today's world of work. The united efforts that placed man on the moon exemplify the efforts being undertaken to coordinate individual, social, and industrial needs.

Occupational Statistics

Used well, one effective tool for occupational planning that gives direction to the training of workers is statistics, available from several sources.

Every ten years, the Bureau of the Census collects data during census week on every person living in the United States and its territories. Included in the findings are the number of workers, where and how they are employed, and how much they earn. From census data available through the United States Department of Commerce, the Department of Labor through the Bureau of Statistics compiles meaningful studies and tables related to specific topics published in reports such as these: *Employment Patterns for 1960-1975, Occupations Engaging the Largest Number of Women, Technology and Manpower in the Health Sciences, 1968-1975*. To make the data more readily usable, a catalogue of the U.S. Government Printing Office is issued annually. It describes the contents of all current reports.

Between regular censuses, monthly and annually the Bureau of the Census obtains data for the United States as a whole through its Current Population Survey (CPS). This sampling survey enables agencies to make projected studies.

Other federal agencies such as the Interstate Commerce Commission, the Statistics Division of the U.S. Civil Service Commission, and the Department of Agriculture collect and issue yearly data on the number of workers in their fields. To estimate future membership needs, professional societies, labor unions, and employee associations also gather membership figures.

The Bureau of Labor Statistics (in the Department of Labor) has translated figures from the census on workers and their earnings in a helpful, almost exciting way showing trends in the labor market and prognosis for the labor force. So significant are these projections that they are used continuously in labor-management contracts, in appraisal of both current and long term trends in wages, and in planning for manpower development and recruitment. Meaningful pamphlets such as *The Working Life for Men* and *The Working Life for Women* indicate the possibilities of turnover, replacement, and mobility.

Each month the Bureau of Labor Statistics publishes the *Employment and Earnings and Monthly Report in the Labor Force*. Each quarter, it releases the *Occupational Outlook*

Quarterly, a projected growth based on the latest compiled figures. Every two years, the results of the occupational outlook research program are published in a comprehensive reference book illustrated with photographs and charts covering more than 700 occupations. Each occupational report covers the employment trends and outlook, the training and education required, and the earnings and working conditions. As background for the different occupations, introductory chapters describe the major trends in population and employment. In addition to these valuable publications, special reports, released periodically, include such titles as these: *Labor Force Projections for 1970-1980*, *Employment and Earnings for States and Areas, 1936-1965*, and *Educational Attainment of Workers*.

The Industrial Structure

When surveying the changing world by analyzing statistics, there are two areas of concern for you as a prospective worker — industrial structure and occupational standings.

For the sake of convenience, common governmental practice has divided the work of the world into nine major industries:

1. Agriculture, the oldest, includes the products of food and fiber.

2. Mining refers to the extraction of minerals from the ground.

3. Contract Construction encompasses the building of houses, offices, schools, bridges, or highways.

4. Manufacturing implies the production, in factories generally, of steel, furniture, machinery, automobiles, and other articles.

5. Transportation and public utilities includes methods of transporting man or goods. Its importance has resulted in the new Department of Transportation.

6. Trade comprises wholesale and retail activities, from local to international.

7. Finance, insurance, and real estate cover the fields implicit in the title. This industry offers relatively little employment but it is growing rapidly in the work of the 20th century.

8. Service includes maintenance, repairs, advertising, domestic, hotel and laundry services, the entertainment fields, private hospitals, and private educational and recreational facilities.

9. Government at national, state, and local levels includes all public education, public health and hospital facilities, sanitation, and police services as well as the executive, legislative, and judicial branches of the government.

The first four major industries as a group are known as the goods-producing sector; the rest are termed service-producing industries. For many years the goods-producing segment dominated the service in both the number of workers employed and in invested capital, but after becoming even with goods production in the 1950's, the service-producing industries moved out ahead in 1965. The prognosis for 1980 is that the number of jobs in the service-producing area will be twice as great as in the goods-producing sector. (1)

In addition to this sweeping forecast, there are other pertinent trends in the industrial structure.

1. Although output is constantly rising, agriculture, which once employed over one-half of all workers, now uses fewer than 6 per cent.

2. Mining employment is steadily and rapidly declining.

3. Construction is expanding and will continue to do so with a growing population and economy.

4. With the burgeoning defense and space demands, manufacturing continues to employ most workers.

5. With new inventions, transportation and public utilities have enlarged and changed. Specifically, the tre-

mendous growth in air and bus travel has offset the decline in the railroad.

6. Trade has been stimulated by the growth of large urban centers and by a rising standard of living. As in the past, future employment growth will require part-time workers, particularly women and young people.

7. Banking is making large percentage gains in employees, along with other financial groups.

8. The service industries, serving both the young and old who need health, medical, and recreation facilities, are growing rapidly.

9. Although the federal government is remaining constant, state and local governments are experiencing great demands for their services. Already more than one out of every six non-farm wage and salary workers are government employees. Teaching and fire and police protection account for the large number of persons needed.

Though labor percentages in an industry may decline, jobs will be available. The industry will still need to accommodate a rising population and an expanding technology.

Occupational Standings

To analyze the world of work, the occupational distribution of workers is equally as important as the size of the industries. Occupations, of course, cut across industrial lines. An accountant may work for the government, an industry, or his own accounting firm. A nurse may work in a hospital, school, or industry, or have her own private practice. In each instance, the *industry* describes where one works, and the *occupation*, what one does.

The rapid change in the nature of industries is matched by the changing demand for workers. In the past, workers have been grouped into four classes: white collar, blue collar, service, and farm workers.

Table 1 Employment in the Service Producing and Goods Producing Industries

Actual 1968/Estimated 1980
The number of workers in the millions

Industrial Sectors	1968	1980	Percentage Increase
Service Producing	44.2	59.5	35%
Government	11.8	16.8	42%
Transportation and public utilities	4.3	4.7	10%
Trade	14.1	18.2	25%
Finance	3.4	4.3	25%
Services	10.6	15.6	50%
Goods Producing	27.5	30.	10%
Manufacturing	19.8	21.9	11%
Contract Construction	3.3	4.6	40%
Mining	0.61	.5	−10%
Agriculture	3.8	3.04	−21%

Data from U.S. Department of Labor, Bureau of Labor Statistics, *Occupational Outlook Handbook* (Washington, D.C.: Government Printing Office, 1970), pp. 11-15.

For the decade of the 1970's, the forecast is that the workers in the white-collar occupations will continue their rapid growth; workers in the blue-collar occupations will be slower than average in most of the occupations; service occupations will increase and farm workers will experience a further decline. Some authorities believe that by 1980, white-collar jobs will account for more than one-half of all employed workers. Total employment is expected to increase about 25 percent between 1968 and 1980. In comparison, an increase of about 36 percent is expected for white-collar occupations. See Table 2.

Table 2 Employment by Major Occupational Group

Actual 1968/Estimated 1980
The number of workers in the millions

Occupational Group	1968	1980	Percentage Increase
White collar workers	35.5	43.5	36%
Professional and technical	10.3	15.1	50%
Proprietary and managerial	7.8	9.3	20%
Clerical	12.8	17.	33%

Table 2   Employment by Major Occupational Group (Cont.)

Sales	4.6	6.	30%
Blue collar workers	29.6	31.5	13%
Craftsmen	10.	12.5	25%
Operatives	14.	15.4	10%
Laborers	3.6	3.6	0%
Service	9.4	13.2	40%
Farm	3.5	2.6	−35%

Data from U.S. Department of Labor, Bureau of Labor Statistics, *Occupational Outlook Handbook* (Washington, D.C.: Government Printing Office, 1970), pp. 15-17.

Under the blue-collar occupations, however, by 1980 the need for craftsmen will increase by 25 percent and operatives in the blue-collar occupations will still be the largest single group in the nation's work force. See Table 3 for the skilled occupations that have more than a hundred thousand workers.

Table 3   Employment of Skilled Workers

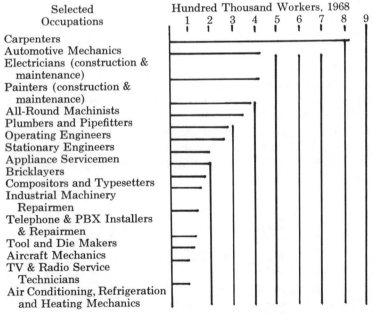

U.S. Dept. of Labor, Bureau of Labor Statistics, *Occupational Outlook Handbook* (Washington, D.C.: Government Printing Office, 1970), p. 349.

The latest figures given in percentages for both industry growth and occupational change predicated for the decade of the seventies are pictured in Table 4 and Table 5.

Table 4 Employment Growth in Industry

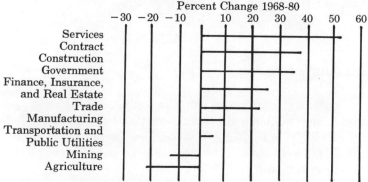

U.S. Dept. of Labor, Bureau of Labor Statistics, *Occupational Outlook Handbook* (Washington, D.C.: Government Printing Office, 1970), p. 13.

Table 5 Occupational Growth and Education Attained

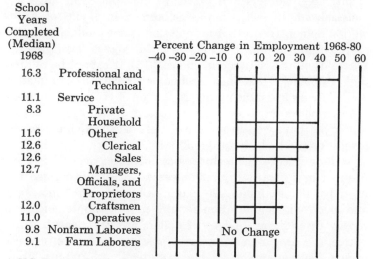

U.S. Dept. of Labor, Bureau of Labor Statistics, *Occupational Outlook Handbook* (Washington, D.C.: Government Printing Office, 1970), p. 16.

These figures are for the purpose of giving you a general idea of the work world and the kinds of workers that are a part of it. As you become more aware of the sector that most interests you and the occupational activity that best suits you, you will wish to investigate and analyze those particular areas for the possibilities of employment.

Automation

Extensive changes in employment needs have been created by automation and cybernation, thus business and industry suddenly have found new workers in the forms of the automated machine and the electronic computer. How will this change affect you?

As early as 1961, dire predictions were being made of the effect of automation on employment. According to one estimate, about 25,000 jobs are eliminated every week by automation. (2) As the years have passed, however, predictions of displaced workers and extensive unemployment have not materialized. In fact, Charles Silberman in *Myths of Automation* demonstrates that automation is not producing unemployment and argues that the new technology is "enlarging the sphere of human action and choice." (3) It cannot be refuted that automation and new technology have brought man a powerful new assistant in the production of goods and services, yet this new apprentice must be regarded with apprehension.

What have we learned in the past decade about this new revolutionary tool of mankind?

Undoubtedly, the technological advances themselves have resulted in a variety of new processes with their corresponding jobs. For example, television, electronic data processing, and electronic computation require proper maintenance and repair. In addition, billions of dollars are being spent on research and development to make possible more extensive use of new discoveries. One authority states that 3,200 new products, including the mighty transistor, are a result of space research programs alone. (4) Today, thousands of men and women are working in fields that were little known only a decade ago — cryogenics, bionics, ultrasonics, and microelectronics.

Remember, however, that the impact of technology on agriculture resulted in improvement in production with considerably fewer workers. In the automobile industry, also, with the use of automated machinery, 17 per cent fewer workers can produce the same number of cars in one year as in former years. Over all, about two million jobs a year are affected by some technological change, requiring people holding those jobs to make some kind of change, such as adjustments to a new job or retraining. (5) With automation, jobs requiring little skill or those repetitive in nature are disappearing because more training and education are demanded to run the automated machinery. Note in Table 5 the level of education attained.

Typical is the story the state employment official told about how a young man came into his office to inquire about the possibilities of a job:

"What can you do?" the official asked.

"Anything," replied the youth.

"But we no longer have anything jobs," the man was forced to reply.

Under automation, the nature of work and jobs seems to require a person with learning experiences that enable him to be maneuverable and adaptable to emerging needs rather than narrowly specialized. A personnel manager in a large electronics company emphasized, "We do not need students trained in a unique way for a specific job. We want imaginative, resourceful, and flexible persons who have a broad background of education and training to enable them to be creative and adaptable."

Certain other factors influencing employment needs provide reasons for optimism. For example, when electronic data processing has been widely installed in banks, the volume of business has grown to the extent that banking employment has continued to rise. During the seventies, the Department of Labor predicts these changes: "Workers will be in sharp demand as the nation explores new approaches to education, bends great effort toward American socio-economic progress, urban renewal, transportation, harnessing the ocean, enhancing the beauty of the land, and conquering outer space." (6) The Report of the Joint Economic Committee to the Senate ended with the words: "Finally, the committee cannot agree that automation and increasing productivity will shrink the need for a dynamic, growing, and better trained work force. Quite the contrary, unmet human and environmental needs are great and will remain so for years to come." (7)

Population Change

Another aspect of change affecting the world of work is the change in population. The great increase in the number of both young and old people has resulted in a shift in the demand for goods and services. In addition, with improved transportation and communication, people have been moving from one part of the country to another, from rural living to urban life, and from one state to another. During the past decade, over 3,000,000 people migrated to California alone. Due to population growth, there was a 22 per cent increase in the size of the work force in the United States, but the Far West's labor force went up by 36 per cent and the Northeast's by only 16 per cent.

People move to areas of high economic opportunities. Counties where family incomes were at the poverty level have now lost half their young adults. As people move into an area, there is an increasing need for goods, services, government, and education. In 1965, one out of every six jobs in the United States was located in California, Texas, and Florida.

The Challenge

You may be asking yourself this: "Is this changing world, more mechanized and mobile than ever before, a better one?"

Some persons think so. Gerard Piel, president and publisher of *Scientific American*, voiced his optimism:

> Work that can be done by machines is either too dull, repetitive, demanding, dangerous, or degrading for human beings; it is better done by machines. The liberation of people from such servitude should set them free for the exercise of their more recognizably human capacities. . .
>
> Inevitably, the transition to this latest phase of human evaluation must bring our values and our institutions into crisis. . . . We are learning in our day that the well being of one man can increase only with the increases in the well being of all men. The ancient habit of truth seeking has disclosed the noblest and most generous aims to human life and (with them) placed in our hands the means to accomplish those ends on earth. (8)

It took the words of a poet to describe the feeling and thoughts of Frank Borman and James Lovell when their spacecraft came around the far side of the moon and they saw, 230,000 miles away, the earth rise.

> To see the earth as it truly is, small and blue and beautiful in that eternal silence where it floats, is to see ourselves as riders on the earth together, brothers on that bright loneliness in the eternal cold — brothers who know now they are truly brothers. (9)

For Exploration and Discussion

1. What is the relationship between urban spread and inner city slums?

2. What justification is there for the black man's demand for a given percentage of employment in plants and institutions?

3. Evaluate the ways in which the disadvantaged are fighting to improve their living conditions.

4. Support your position on violence by a minority group as a means of obtaining economic advantage.

5. Recently, Robert Heilbroner wrote, "The needs and wants of our own society may well be passing beyond the era in which private requirements were to be placed above all other considerations, into a new time when public needs will have to rank as high as, or even above, the demands of the private buyer." List public needs which should take priority over private needs.

6. What persons do you know who have been discharged from their jobs by automation?
   What businesses do you know that have installed automatic devices? What has been the effect on the number of employed?

7. For diversion and perhaps hope, man has dreamed of utopias and planned ways to actualize them. What would your own utopia be like? Is there any relationship between utopia and automation?

8. Study the provisions of the Educational Opportunity Act and the Economic Opportunity Act. Has your state supported these programs?

9. To observe changes taking place in your community, with another member of your class visit the offices in your area of one of the following:
       New industries   Head Start Program
       Urban Renewal   Newspaper publishing company
       City Planning   College Placement
       State Employment Office
   Plan your observation before the visit and discuss your plans in class.

10. Read the first three chapters in the latest *Occupational Outlook Handbook* (Washington D.C.: U.S. Government Printing

Office) for recent statistics compiled by the Department of Labor on trends in employment.

11. Investigate the tapes on careers available in your library. Provide for a time during the semester to listen to as many as you can that have any interest for you.

References

1. Seymour Wolfbein, *Occupational Information* (New York: Random House, 1968), p. 44.

2. Max Baer and Edward C. Roeber, *Occupational Information,* 3rd edition (Chicago: Science Research Associates, Inc., 1964), p. 51.

3. Charles E. Silberman, *The Myths of Automation* (New York: Harper & Row, 1968), p. 114.

4. S. B. Childs, "Is the Work Ethic Realistic in an Age of Automation?" Peters and Hansen, eds., *Vocational Guidance and Career Development* (New York: Macmillan Company, 1966), pp. 3-12.

5. Wolfbein, *Occupational Information,* p. 90.

6. *Occupational Outlook Handbook* (Washington, D.C.: U.S. Government Printing Office, 1966-67), p. 16.

7. *Report of the Joint Economic Committee,* Report No. 1568, 1968.

8. Gerard Piel, Address before the 1964 Conference of the Association for Higher Education. Chicago, April, 1964. Reprinted by permission of the author.

9. Archibald MacLeish, "A Reflection." © 1968, The New York Times Company. Reprinted by permission.

Part II
The Basis of Choice

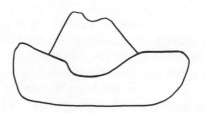

5

Whose Choice?

Who can choose for you? Who selects your food and clothes? Who can choose your friends? Who can make your choice of work?

As you think about these questions, you will realize, of course, that they are personal ones. Only you can know your own tastes and preferences; it is absurd to think of anyone else choosing for you. But for some of you there may be a nagging concern that possibly someone else may be doing your choosing. Growing up is not easy; it is a slow task involving many decisions.

Parental Influence

When you begin to plan your career, you may find that your parents are interested and highly involved. Some parents find in their children's job selection a chance to make up for their own failures or their own lack of opportunity. Perhaps they seek to extend their social position or to meet neighbors' expectations. But most parents intend to be helpful and prevent you from making mistakes. For parents, too, your growing up is often painful.

When they urge a specific career choice, sometimes parents ignore clues that could indicate suitable work. Bob, Bill, and Everett had to make choices with parental influence.

....

Bob's Failure   Bob's father was a well-known attorney in a large downtown office. He ignored the fact that his son had graduated from high school with a C— average although he had received a grade of A in the one shop course he had taken. Bob's scores on his entrance tests to the junior college were low, his highest score being in mathematics.

When Bob consulted his counselor to arrange his college program, he expressed a desire to go into electronics. As a result, courses for the electronics program were selected.

The following morning, when the counselor arrived at her office, Bob was at the door accompanied by a well-dressed, middle-aged man whom he introduced as his father. The father quickly explained that he was dissatisfied with his son's college program; that he wished him to take a liberal arts program. The counselor explained that she realized that both of them were interested in the young man's welfare but the choice of program was actually the student's. She turned to Bob and asked, "What program do you wish to enroll in, Bob?"

Bob hesitated, glanced at his father and replied, "I'll take the liberal arts course."

Bob was a hard worker and he studied in earnest. But two months later he stuck his head in the counselor's door, with a big grin on his face, and stated, "I'm failing!"

Bill   Bill's mother insisted that Bill could do anything if he tried hard enough. Because his older brother was ill, Bill tried to accommodate her. It took him three years of making C and D grades before he could accept the fact that his career was not dentistry.

Everett   Everett liked mechanics. His tests pointed up the appropriateness of his choice. But Everett's father, a city official, could not entirely accept Everett's decision. Then he made arrangements for Everett to go into partnership with a garage owner. To own his own business made being a mechanic an acceptable career from the father's point of view. Fortunately, Everett was happy, too.

....

Social Influence

Society's influence on your choice of careers is subtle. Reverence for money, power, and prestige is part of Americana. It is expressed in the newspaper, on TV, at the movies. Your friends, your family, and your instructors often suggest careers which have status. And you listen.

Very few persons would not enjoy money, power, and prestige. But are these criteria for choosing a career? For some of you the answer may be "yes." For most of you these rewards may be far down on the list.

Your choice of your job is yours, but this does not mean you should not ask questions or seek suggestions. Listening to parents and to others in the society in which you live is proper. You will receive some good advice and even some wisdom.

....

Poon's School   Poon, a brilliant foreign student, said to his counselor, "It is so difficult to get into a medical school, I think I'll change my major from medicine to engineering."

"What does your country need most?" asked the counselor.

"Medicine," replied Poon.

"If medicine is what you truly wish, investigate every possible medical school," advised the counselor.

A few years later Poon appeared at the counselor's office. "Thank you for insisting that I be a doctor," he said with a twinkle in his eyes, "I have my acceptance into a good medical school in Canada."

....

When Alice, wandering in Wonderland, asked the Cheshire Cat how to get out of the woods, he replied, "That depends on where you want to go."

To determine where you want to go, you must know where you are and who you are. The next five chapters will help you take a careful look at yourself. The faceless man is a sad sight. In *The Trial*, the hero cannot see his accusers; he only knows that he is being tried by his inner self.

Identity and Choice

Psychologists are aware that in the second decade of life youth faces the real world with some ability to understand it. This new insight into reality is accompanied by great energy, drive, and capability.

To find your own identity, you must face the real world and explore it. You must discover what you can do and how well you do it. You must build things — cars, boats, racers, stereos. You must pit your physical strength against your peers in football, swimming, and mountain climbing. You must earn money and make friends. You must organize and master whatever you can. Such seeing, exploring, and doing must be of your own choosing. Then society, too, will observe what you can do and who you are and what you are becoming. Meanwhile, you will be finding your way and your personal identity.

Erik Eriksen, an authority on human development, explains the process of finding and establishing identity:

> Let us take our time in saying it . . . [because it is] complex and it is weighty. . . . Identity is found in the core of the individual and yet also in the core of his community. . . . It is a process of interaction between the two. In psychological terms, the individual reflects and observes: he judges himself in the light of what he perceives to be the way others judge him in comparison to themselves and their . . . [expectations]; and, in turn, he judges their way of judging him in the light of how he perceives himself in comparison to them and his . . . [expectations]. . . . The process is always developing and is a process of increasing differentiation in the widening circle of the community and of the world. (1)

But we must remember that in youth, identity formation reaches a crisis. Decisions must be made, often unconsciously, of "whom you will serve" and on what terms you will live.

....

Jon's Freedom   Jon explained that he was taking fewer units this semester because he had to take a job. "I wanted to move in with a couple of the fellows," he stated. "It isn't that my parents wanted me to leave. They think I am foolish because I could live at home free. But they have their ideas of how I should cut my hair and the kind of clothes I should wear. They are impressed because I'm good in mathematics and they want me to be an engineer. But I think engineering is boring. I feel free to be what I want to be now that I am on my own."

....

....

Sandra   It isn't always necessary to leave home in order to assert your developing identity.

Sandra found while attending junior college that living at home could be satisfactory. Because she earned some of her expenses in a part-time job, she discovered that it was possible to relate to her parents on a different level. She tried showing an interest in her family and found that they treated her in the same way.

....

Identity formation takes place on all levels of mental functioning. When Thomas Carlyle suffered a severe spiritual crisis, he spent three weeks in total sleeplessness. During that time, he reports, he cast out the spirit of "negation" and "whining," and became a "fiery," committed human being.

Protesting young people are seeking identity as they reject the stereotyped "clean cut" and "clean shaven" organization man. In many cases, they are searching for new ways of facing up to what truly counts.

> Franklin Murphy, Chancellor at the University of California at Los Angeles writes: I visited some young people in Chile who were Peace Corps volunteers. They were living in a slum clearance area on the outskirts of Santiago. They lived in a hovel, exactly like the 150,000 people living in the district. There was a young couple, graduates of Emory University, and a Negro boy. They worked hard and were serious about their job. They had fixed objectives and were making social and political judgments. They were beginning to relate the isolated experiences of this slum district in Chile to the state of the world and the state of American society, and they were thinking what they were going to do about it. The desires of these three young people are not specific in terms of the great American precedent which is to sell shoes on Main Street. Or to run Dad's drug store. They're thinking about the important issues of our times and how they can bring this revolutionary society even more into focus, where the old kinds of commitments and objectives no longer fit or have meaning. (2)

Identity has a particular meaning also for persons of a minority race. Minority groups are demanding, rightfully, that their identity be respected and not repressed by the white man.

During the first two years of college an *identity crisis* often occurs. A student is tested in at least three different areas: he is tested in his ability to achieve what others are achieving; he is tested in his ability to accept new friends and new ideas; and he is tested in his ability to meet his own ideas about himself. When you consider that 50 per cent of the students enrolled in college drop out the first two years, it is clear that some conflicting ideas about themselves must be resolved.

....

Henry's Crisis   Henry's father was a successful druggist and a popular man in his community of 20,000 people. Henry and his father were good pals, and the entire family situation was wholesome and stabilizing in its influence on the members.

Henry worked in his father's store on weekends and during vacations and made many acquaintances with doctors. These and other contacts gave him a strong interest in medicine. In his third year of high school, he definitely decided on medicine as a career and took the high school courses necessary for a college major in pre-medicine. His grades were consistently "B's" in mathematics and science.

Henry was a good-looking young man and an excellent golfer. He was active in class and student body organizations. His vocational plans were well known to all his friends and friends of his family. He played golf with a number of doctors to whom he related his plans to study medicine. The doctors encouraged him in his chosen field of work.

Henry graduated from high school without ever having taken any scholastic aptitude and achievement tests to determine how his capacities measured up to the demands of a college pre-medical course. When he enrolled in college, he stated that medicine was his objective, and his adviser signed him up for the usual program of chemistry, zoology, German and English. He also was given a battery of tests during orientation week which unfortunately were not scored until after he had signed up for his courses.

As soon as he got into these college classes, he began to realize that he was pursuing an objective which was beyond his abilities. He fought the battle for ten weeks and then, under great pressure, decided to quit college and enter military service. When asked why he was withdrawing, he offered the explanation that he was uncertain about his vocational choice and that he thought a few years in the Army would enable him to find out what he really wanted to do. He did not contact a counselor until after he had signed up for military service and so it was impossible for him to change his plans.

In looking over his college entrance test scores, it appeared that he did not exceed the 30th percentile on any of the tests involving mathematics and physical science. Henry's self-concept received a severe blow in his first semester of college. This was a very critical time in his life. It was unfortunate that in high school he had not checked his objective against his capacities. Likewise, in college, his adviser should have given him this information. The blow to his self-esteem was so great that he could not bring himself to seek aid when he saw he was failing. (3)

....

The pressures on such a young man in a small community can be very disturbing when his well-publicized plans have to be revised.

Finding your Way

To make your own choices you must know who you are, at least in part, and accept who you are, as much as is possible. Not that anyone ever achieves complete personal insight, but there must be more knowing and more accepting for better choosing.

Accepting one's limitations can be very painful. T. S. Eliot states in the play *The Cocktail Party*, "All life is an endless

struggle to think well of oneself." If you have decided that you must be something you are not, in order to think well of yourself, then you must take a careful look at your value system. Therefore, your value system will be discussed in the next chapter.

For Exploration and Discussion

1. Evaluate the choices that are now open to you in education or experiences that will affect your working career; in contrast, decide what choices are closed to you.

2. What has had a strong influence on your career choice up to this time? How does your father's work affect your choice? Research the relationship between father and son career choices.

3. How specific should your career choice be during your first two years of college? How permanent should any career choice be?

4. Do you know anyone who is in the wrong field of work? Why is it wrong? What historical figures or prominent characters have made poor career choices?

5. One form of alienation is alienation from oneself. In the past decade, many writers have been concerned with the problem of personal identity. For further exploration of this problem, read *Man for Himself* by Erich Fromm, *Motivation and Personality* by Abraham Maslow, or *The Lonely Crowd* by David Riesman.

6. By what subtle specific traits do you identify the personalities of your friends, your instructors, yourself?

7. Develop a program for creative self-action and experiment with it.

References

1. Eric Eriksen, *Identity, Youth and Crisis* (New York: W. W. Norton & Co., 1968), pp. 22-24.

2. Franklin D. Murphy, "The Time-Honored Student Restlessness," *Intercollegian,* Orientation, Summer 1967, p. 12.

3. Hugh M. Bell, "Ego-Involvement in Vocational Decisions," *Personnel and Guidance Journal,* July 1960, pp. 732-35.

6

Your Value System

A speaker at a recent college commencement told the following story:

> At a graduation party that I attended, one of the girls present had received a new sports car for a graduation gift. As the evening wore on, one of the guests asked her if he might drive her car; she gave her consent and a few minutes later the car pulled out with a harsh grinding of gears. Members of the party flinched and glanced at the owner, whereupon the girl smiled, shrugged her shoulders and said, "Cars are for people."
>
> Those of us who came up through the Great Depression and had to scrape and save to buy material things took pride in protecting and preserving them. But the girl is right. Cars are for people. And those of you who have grown up with two bathrooms instead of one, or none, have had to remind us that always people are more important than things. We thank you for that. (1)

Young people are questioning the value system of our society with relentless and thorough scrutiny. When you ask certain questions, we have to hang our heads. "Why in a democratic society, do we have obvious discrimination?" "Why in a peace-loving society, are we bombing others?" "Why do educators chiefly talk about things?" "Why are grades in school so important and so irrelevant?" Of course, the answer is, "You have to be realistic. That is the way it always has been." But aware youth are shaking their heads, saying, "No, it's time to change."

If you have already begun to question the value systems of those around you, you may also have begun to ask yourself what values, what deep-seated beliefs you live by.

Your Value System

What do we mean by a value system? How does it differ from a moral standard or ethical behavior?

A *moral standard* reflects the generally accepted value system a given group may hold whereas an *ethical standard* states the ideal values the group has approved. The moral standard and the ethical standard may be at variance. For example, the Declaration of Human Rights is an attempt to make real the ethical beliefs of all nations; the differing divorce laws demonstrate varying moral standards. In its laws a nation may reflect moral values; in its religious writings, its ethics.

"On what do you place value?" "When are you happiest?" "What makes life worth living for you?" These questions are not easily answered. There are, of course, no right or wrong answers, and the final outcome is your personal commitment.

Some persons can feel comfortable only when they are wearing fine clothes or driving an expensive car. To repudiate material values and to socialize or create is important to others; a Thoreau or Van Gogh must sacrifice materialism and social life for wisdom or art. The scientist's dedication is legendary and the scholar's devotion is even decried, but each has chosen what he values most and each fulfills a social purpose.

It is not easy to determine truthfully your own value system. Often it is a painful and slow discovery. By comparing your behavior and choices with those of your friends and co-workers, you gain some idea of the values which guide you. When you develop greater independence and assume more responsibility for crucial decisions, you also strengthen the values in which you believe.

In addition to your personal experience and self-evaluation, you may take the "Study of Values" test developed by Allport, Vernon, and Lindzey. This test brings your beliefs into focus with career choices. The answers to the test questions are weighted on a scale of three and include questions such as these:

1. Would modern society benefit more from (a) more concern for the rights and welfare of citizens; (b) greater knowledge of the fundamental laws of human behavior?

2. If you were engaged in an industrial organization and, assuming salaries to be equal, would you prefer to work (a) as a counselor for employees; (b) in an administrative position?

The resulting scores are grouped into five categories of value choices.

Theoretical:
> Developing ideas in the area of discovering truth rather than making judgments.

Aesthetic:
> Appreciation of beauty and appropriateness.

Economic:
> Making money and doing what is practical.

Altruistic:
> A love of people in the sense of a concern for their social welfare and a generosity in helping others.

Religious:
> Seeking to understand the philosophic and spiritual aspects of life.

Although you may have more than one high value score, most students have a varying profile with one score higher than the rest.

Values and Career Choice

How do personal values influence career choices? How do values affect one's success in and liking for work? How can a conscious understanding of your own value system help you in your choice of a career?

An extensive research study about undergraduate career decisions sampled students from 135 colleges. Over 50,000 students participated in the study to determine how many changes in career plans occur, what the changes are, and why they are made. (2) For purposes of the study, careers were grouped into the following areas: the natural sciences, the social sciences, the fine arts, education, engineering, and the professions.

Approximately one-half of the students reported a shift in career plans. One of the ideas behind the research was the belief that occupational choices are made in such a way that a person's values will correspond to the values that can be realized in his work. This hypothesis seemed to be substantiated by the following results:

1. People-oriented or service-oriented (altruistic) students changed from the social sciences and humanities to education and the professions, primarily when the service-oriented students realized that the social sciences and humanities are cerebral in nature.

2. Students who valued the opportunity to be original and creative changed from business into the sciences and humanities.

3. Students whose fundamental interest was in making money shifted to business, law, and engineering.

By their senior year, the students had taken definite positions. See Table 6 on page 58.

As a consequence of these changes, the nine fields other than the biological sciences are distributed at graduation about the clock and their predominant values—the ones that differentiate them from students in general—are brought into relief.

**Table 6   Values Students Held at Graduation in Relation
to their Final Choice of Major**

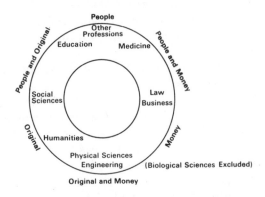

Reprinted from the study in James A. Davis, *Undergraduate Career Decisions* (Chicago: Aldine Publishing Company); copyright © 1965 by National Opinion Research Center, p. 61.

Of course, the conclusions drawn from this study do not mean that everyone in business or law would do anything for money, and that teachers do not value being well paid. Rather they suggest that the top priority in your scheme of personal values will be a significant factor in your career choice.

What is valued by everyone is work that is useful and worthy so that a man may feel that his industry counts; that his job is necessary and requires his best capacities; and that it can be done with honor and dignity.

Paul Goodman, who says, "It is hard to grow up when there isn't enough man's work," cites some examples:

Consider a likely job. A youth who is alert and willing chooses for auto mechanics. That's a good job, familiar to him; he often watched them as a kid. It's careful and dirty at the same time. In a small garage it's sociable; one can talk to the customers (girls). You please people in trouble by fixing their cars and a man is pleased to see rolling out on its own the car that limped in behind the tow truck. The pay is as good as the next fellow's who is respected.

So our young man takes this first-rate job. But what when he learns that the cars have built-in obsolescence; that the manufacturers do not want them to be repaired or repair-

able? They have lobbied for a law that requires them to provide spare parts for only five years. (It used to be ten).
Repairing the new cars is often a matter of cosmetics, not
mechanics; and the repairs are pointlessly expensive. The
insurance rate, therefore, doubles and trebles on old and new
cars alike. Gone are the days of keeping the jalopies in good
shape, the artist-work of a proud mechanic. But everybody
is paying for foolishness for, in fact, the new models are only
trivially superior; the whole thing is a sell.

It is hard for a young man to maintain his feeling of
justification, sociability, serviceability. It is not surprising if
he quickly becomes cynical and time-serving, interested in a
fast buck. And so, on the *Reader's Digest* test, the investi-
gators (coming in with a disconnected coil wire) found that
63 per cent of the mechanics charged for repairs they didn't
make, and lucky if they didn't also take out the new fuel
pump and replace it with a used one. (65 per cent of radio
repair shops, but only 49 per cent of watch repairmen lied,
overcharged, or gave false diagnoses . . .)

Most manual jobs do not lend themselves so readily to
knowing the facts and fraudulently taking advantage oneself. . . . Even so, there is evidence of the same disbelief in
the enterprise as a whole, with a resulting attitude of profound indifference. . . .

The worst comment of all would be — "During my productive years I will spend eight hours a day doing what is
no good." (3)

Personal Responsibility

Work can be a personal commitment to meaningful activity, the opposite of Lewis Carroll's lesson in futility:

First, the Dodo marked out a race course, in a sort of
circle, and then all the party were placed along the course,
here and there. There was no "one, two, three, and away!"
but they began running when they liked, and left off when
they liked, so that it was not easy to know when the race was
over. However, when they had been running half an hour or
so, the Dodo suddenly called out, "The race is over!" and
they all crowded round him, panting and asking, "But who
won?" (4)

Fortunately, in a world of work, a man's life is still his own. His approach to his job is his own. To make "the laborer worthy of his hire" is his responsibility.

For Exploration and Discussion

1. What jobs could you accept with impunity? What jobs would you be proud of having?

2. If you believe war is immoral, what should be your attitude toward work in defense industries?

3. To what extent are your personal values influenced by society's ethics?

4. If idealism is incompatible with reality, is it practical to speak of having values?

5. How are your values different from your friends? Your parents?

6. Compare the values of persons over and under 30. Is the difference a generation gap or individual differences?

7. Test your value system by taking the Allport, Vernon, Lindzey "Study of Values" examination.

8. Kenneth Keniston of Yale Medical School has written two profound books on youth in American society. For understanding the alienation of young people from the mainstream of society, read chapters 2 through 7 in *The Uncommitted* (New York:

Dell Publishing Company, 1965). For understanding the motivation of young activists read *The Young Radicals* (New York: Harcourt, Brace & World, 1968), Chapters 4-8.

References

1. Snell Putney, professor of sociology, San Jose State College, from a commencement address given at San Jose City College.

2. James A. Davis, *Undergraduate Career Decisions* (Chicago: Aldine Publishing Company, 1965); copyright © 1965 by National Opinion Research Center, pp. 31-37. Reprinted with permission from the publisher and the author.

3. Paul Goodman, *Growing Up Absurd* (New York: Random House, 1960), pp. 19-20. Reprinted with permission from the publisher.

4. Charles Dodgson, *The Complete Works of Lewis Carroll* (New York: Modern Library, Random House, n.d.), pp. 37-38.

7

What Tests Tell You

Some questions you may ask of counselors, parents, and fellow students are these:

"What am I fitted for?" "What am I able to do?" "How smart am I?" "What is my IQ?" "What am I like?" "How do I compare with others?"

And, of course, you want exact answers. You may feel that if you get the word, much of your uncertainty will disappear. Tests can help you answer your questions, although they cannot give you complete and exact answers. But many reliable and varied tests that are now available can be used to determine your aptitudes and interests in comparison with others.

Aptitude Tests

Entrance examinations taken for acceptance into college are a kind of intelligence test, usually divided into several areas. In order to be accepted in many universities you must achieve stated minimum scores on individual tests or an accepted combination of scores. Girls generally make higher scores on verbal tests and lower scores on mathematical or quantitative tests.

A standard entrance test for many colleges and universities is the *Scholastic Aptitude Test* (SAT), which is a three-hour objective test designed to measure your verbal and mathematical skills. It is offered by the College Entrance Examination Board, a nonprofit membership organization that provides tests and other educational services for schools and colleges. The College Board also offers achievement tests in various subjects which you may take the same day as the SAT if the college you plan to attend requires it.

Another test that many colleges use for their entrance examination is the *American College Test* (ACT) which gives scores in four areas (English, mathematics, social science, and natural science) followed by a composite score. Some colleges, particularly public junior colleges, do not require a minimum score in order to be accepted, but use the scores to supplement high school grades for placement in various courses.

Another entrance test, the *School and College Aptitude Test* (SCAT), is divided into two areas (verbal and quantitative) with a total which is not an average of the two.

The purpose of all these aptitude tests is to determine the ability of a person to succeed in academic work, and in this sense, the tests reveal the intellectual ability of the person taking the test. However, since the questions are related to particular bodies of knowledge, the tests also measure achievement. An individual who has had little or no familiarity with the information being tested will not do well and still may be intelligent.

Intelligence Tests

An intelligence test refers to the intelligence quotient (IQ) or "ability" of the person taking the test. When comparing aptitude tests and IQ tests, it is important to realize that the aptitude test gives scores in different kinds of mental ability, that is, English and mathematics; an IQ test reports mental perception with only one score. That score can then be compared with the average scores made by thousands of others.

The *Otis Quick Scoring Mental Ability Test* and the *Henmon-Nelson Tests of Mental Ability* give the test taker a rough estimate of his IQ. A more nearly valid test of an individual's IQ can be obtained when a test is administered individually by a skilled tester.

One problem with all aptitude and intelligence tests is that the individuals taking them must have come from homes with similar cultural and linguistic backgrounds. If they have not, the scores are not valid. Schools and test centers have gradually become aware that there are other ways to measure intelligence than through a measure of verbal skills, because intelligence may be defined as the capacity to profit by experience or as the ability to solve problems. (1)

Many environmental influences can affect what a person scores on tests. The effect of a classroom environment on children's IQ test scores is highlighted in the book *Pygmalion in the Classroom*, a report of a classroom experiment in South San Francisco, and in *Pygmalion Reconsidered*, an extensive reanalysis of the original data. Teachers were told falsely that certain children in their classes tested higher than the others in their classes, and so possessed higher IQ's. At the end of the term some of those children actually did test higher. An analysis of the changes that took place in these children suggests that for some children a strong, natural teacher expectancy may influence pupil achievement. (2)

....

Minority IQ   A college counselor with a minority background was explaining to his colleagues some of his embarrassments while growing up. Once his sixth grade teacher listed all the children's names on the board with their IQ scores. The lowest three names on the list were obvious because of the characteristic spelling of the minority group. Listed among them was his name.

Someone asked, "Did you feel crushed?"

"Oh, no," he replied, "I didn't believe it. I knew I was much smarter than the kid across the aisle."

....

There are several reasons why test scores are not accurate. The person taking the test may not be well, or he may be anxious, or he may be a poor test taker. Any of these circumstances must be taken into consideration.

You must, however, recognize your own strengths and weaknesses. If your tests reveal that you have an average intellectual ability, you may have to work harder than average to succeed in college. If you doubt your test scores, you can check your ability by your performance in classwork and in other life experiences. Tests are only one of the ways to determine your abilities.

One other fact about IQ should be emphasized. John Stalnaker states it well:

> It is obvious that no one is born educated; no matter how high his intelligence is, he can learn only to the extent that he applies himself. With equal effort the very bright student will learn more than the dull student; but if the person of lesser aptitude works more diligently than the individual with greater intelligence, he may indeed climb higher than his brighter associate who has less ambition and drive. (3)

Experiences on every campus and in every line of work prove that this statement is true.

Interest Tests

Interests are activities which are personally preferred, and can range from "liked very much" to "disliked very much." Interests are feelings of intentness, concern, or curiosity. They can be shallow or deep-seated.

Men's interests change very little from 25 to 55 years of age, some from 20 to 25 years, and much more from 15 to 20 years. The changes taking place between 15 and 20 years usually result in the direction of higher ratings.

Interest tests are not tests at all but inventories of personal interests that are helpful to an individual searching for his line of work. Not only do the scores reveal your interests but they can be compared with those of persons who are successfully engaged in specific lines of work. If your interests are similar to persons who are successful in their field, then you receive a high score for this occupation. In addition, similar kinds of work are placed within a group so that several high scores in that cluster designate an area compatible with your interests.

One of the first interest tests was the *Strong Vocational Interest Blanks* (SVIB), developed in 1927, and since then carefully checked and refined. The SVIB was constructed by testing the interests of men and women who were outstanding in their line of work, and comparing their interests with persons who were in different occupations or who were only average in their work performance. There are different SVIB tests for men and women. Since the women's form contains fewer occupations and has not been subject to extensive longitudinal studies, it is often beneficial for women to take the men's as well as the women's form, particularly if they are entering a profession in which there are many men. (4)

Scores on the SVIB are returned to you on a profile sheet. For each occupation listed, an area designated by dark green symbolizes the interests of the average person. Your interests are marked with a red line and show the relationship of your interests to the average. A mark way above the average implies that your interests are similar to persons who are successful in the field; a mark below implies your interests are unlike persons successful in the field.

To help you interpret your ratings, the following information is provided on the profile sheet:

> An "A" rating means that the individual has the interests of persons successfully engaged in that occupation; a "C" rating means that a person does not have such interests. ... It is seldom that persons with "C" ratings are found in the occupation and, if so engaged, they are either indifferent successes who are likely to drop out or are carrying on the work in some more or less unusual manner.

And this advice is added:

> Occupations rated "A" and "B+" should be carefully considered before definitely deciding against them; occupa-

tions rated "C," "C+," and "B" should be carefully considered before definitely deciding to enter them. (5)

When the SVIB was revised in 1969 to modernize the items, a new section was also added labeled *The Basic Interest Scales*. The upper half of the profile sheet now charts the profile of a person's "likings," a double line shows the average scores of persons tested at age 52, and a single line reveals their scores at age 16. The test taker's score is in red and by comparing his score to these two lines, it is possible to tell how his interest on each item compares to the interest of the average adult or teenager.

In interpreting the Basic Scale score, you should look mainly at the high and low scores, the areas where you differ most from other persons. Usually, but not always, there will be at least one or two high scores and one or two low scores. The task then is to find occupational areas that inherently involve your dominant interests. These scores are valuable because they can suggest directions you may not have considered before, and point to occupations you now can explore and evaluate further.

The *Kuder Preference Record* is another interest inventory that has been in use since 1940. This test has two sections on the same score sheet that show interest levels in various occupations and college majors. This discrimination is useful.

Some vocational counselors give both the Kuder and the Strong because both are helpful in analyzing one's interests. Interpreting interest test scores is not a "cut and dried," "black and white" projection; rather, it takes careful analysis.

"What if I have several high scores?" you may ask. All high ratings should be considered. You may choose one of the occupations rated as "A" or plan to use two or more occupations with high ratings in some career that combines both activities.

....

Utilizing Interests   An example of a student who wished to use all of his varied interests is a student who had "A" ratings in

AUTHOR-JOURNALIST and ADVERTISING MAN; "B+" ratings in FOREST SERVICE MAN; and "B" or "B–" in most of the other occupations in group IV (TECHNICAL AND SKILLED TRADES). Several years later, he reported that he was engaged in publicity work for the National Park Service and thoroughly enjoyed his work. Though his interests were in two unrelated areas, he found an occupation with an opportunity to enjoy both. (5)

Change From Sales   A salesman with high scores in three sales occupations also had high scores in the social service group. When his job required him to high pressure retailers into buying more of his product than they would probably be able to sell, he began to feel guilty and unhappy and he began to lose sales. Therefore he left this job and took another providing personal service to the customer, and he again became successful. He would probably have been successful in public contact work for a non-profit organization. (5)

A brilliant example of a man with many A's and B's on his interest tests (plus high academic ability) is the late Ray Lyman Wilbur, who was a practicing physician, dean of a medical school, President of Stanford University, and Secretary of the Interior. (5)

In most cases of widespread interests, the highest scores are relatively low, all B's and B+'s. Many businessmen fall into this category. Business students shift easily from one major to another. Advancement in pay or position seems to be more important to them than interest in the activity itself. The man with professional interests is quite different. His high scores are typically in one area and he prefers a specific type of activity. Many professionals who have deserted their primary interest for an increase in pay or position have later expressed dissatisfaction. Some have even returned to their original work. (5)

Interests Versus Aptitudes

What about the student who rates "A" in the career of physician, but he has neither the finances nor the ability to pursue this career? The American Medical Association (AMA) states that, for every physician, 12 technicians are needed including pathologists, public health officers, research personnel, physical therapists, occupational therapists, medical assistants, and nurses, among many others. (6) A person truly interested in the medical field could choose the level in which it would be possible for him to function.

In the education field an individual might choose to be administrator, teacher, teacher's aide, nursery school assistant, school secretary or clerk, according to his mental or financial ability to get the necessary education.

In the field of home economics, the individual could choose fashion designer, designer's assistant, textile specialist, fashion model, buyer, and sales person, or many others.

Interest tests must always be interpreted in the light of other tests and the knowledge of the "whole" person. Used in this way they are valuable. It is a maxim that what we are interested in doing, we do well and what we can do well, we will find interesting. So far, researchers say, interests have given a higher prediction of future occupational behavior than any other measure. (7) *strong*

Can we predict what occupation a person will choose because of his interests? Not usually. People have religious, social, and economic beliefs or values which may be considered more important to them than their interests in choosing a satisfactory occupation. In the previous chapter we recognized how values and attitudes identified by the *Study of Values* test may motivate the individual. The correlation between values and interests is frequently greater for the person with business interests because he generally values material gain. The person with interest in the artistic area seems to value the aesthetic, and the person with strong scientific interests most often scores high in theoretical values. The *Study of Values* profile, combined with interest inventories, is useful in analyzing what you are like.

Special Tests

Are you talented? Are there tests to determine your special gifts? Yes, there are. Art majors and engineering majors score high on the *Minnesota Paper Board Form*, a timed twenty-minute test in which the testee must match geometric shapes; the accuracy of his perception of spatial relationships is the basis of success.

The Bennett Mechanical Comprehension Test, available with different tests for men and women, is for entering freshmen in engineering schools.

Highly specialized tests in finger dexterity, musical pitch, clerical skills and other special activities have been constructed to be used primarily for screening applicants in diverse occupational fields.

A *General Aptitude Test Battery* (GATB) developed by the United States Employment Service (USES) consists of twelve individual tests and covers nine aptitude factors representing the abilities required for most industrial occupations. The aptitude factors tested are stated in this manner:

v — verbal	Ability to understand meanings of words and ideas associated with them and to use them effectively. To comprehend language, to understand relationships between words, and to understand meanings of whole sentences and paragraphs. To present information and ideas clearly.
n — numerical	Ability to perform arithmetic operations quickly and accurately.
s — spatial	Ability to comprehend forms in space and understand relationships of plane and solid objects. May be used in such tests as blueprint reading and in solving geometry problems.
p — form perception	Ability to make visual comparisons and discriminations and see slight differences in shapes and shadings of figures and widths and lengths of lines.
q — clerical perception	Ability to perceive differences in copy, to proofread words and numbers, and to avoid errors in arithmetic computation.
k — motor coordination	Ability to coordinate eyes and hands in making precise movements. Ability to make a movement response accurately and quickly.
f — finger dexterity	Ability to move the fingers and manipulate small objects with the fingers rapidly and accurately.

| m — manual dexterity | Ability to work with the hands easily and skillfully in placing and turning motions. |
| g — intelligence | General learning ability. The ability to "catch on" or understand instructions and underlying principles. Ability to reason and make judgments. |

The value of the GATB lies in determining minimum aptitude requirements for persons seeking employment through USES. With special arrangements, the GATB may be taken at your school or college or at the USES office in your city.

Personality Tests

You may be wondering why nothing has been stated about personality tests. There are two reasons: first, personality tests are developed from a medical or psychiatric approach and are most effective for revealing persons who need help in developing more desirable social traits and better adjustment; second, the tests need more refinement to be useful in occupational choice. However, there is one personality test that was created for the purpose of determining personality characteristics of "normal" persons and for use in a school or college setting, the *California Psychological Inventory* (CPI).

The CPI is divided into four broad categories: the first category is concerned with Self-Acceptance, Sociability, and Sense of Well-Being; the second category deals with Tolerance, Responsibility, and Self-Control; the third category measures Independence, Conformity, and Efficiency, and the fourth measures Flexibility and Perceptiveness.

Test Reliability

Test centers and research centers throughout the country are updating tests, refining them, and developing new ones for the purpose of making better predictions of human abilities and potential. The use of the computer is accelerating this refinement, but the scores must be used with the other means of determining what you are like. The weakness of the multiple-choice questions used overwhelmingly on objective-type tests has been pinpointed by Banesh Hoffman in *The Tyranny of Testing*. He makes two valid points: "What sense is there in giving tests in which the candidate just picks answers without any opportunity to give reasons for his choice?" and "Human abilities and potentialities are too complex, too diverse, and too intricately interactive to be measured satisfactorily by present techniques." Hoffman concludes that there is a place for multiple-choice tests, but it is strictly a limited one. (8)

There is nothing sacred about a test score and it must not be worshipped. Of each test, you must ask, "How relevant is what is being asked to what is being tested? How relevant is what is being tested to what I want to know?"

For Exploration and Discussion

1. When possible, take several of the tests described in this chapter.
   a. The Strong Interest Inventory (This should be taken first as it must be sent away to be scored.)
   b. The Kuder Preference Record (This is an effective complement to the Strong and must also be sent away to be scored.)

c. The Allport, Vernon, Lindzey—Study of Values
d. Minnesota Paper Board Form
e. Bennett Mechanical Test
f. The ACT, the SAT, or the SCAT
You have probably taken an aptitude test; if not, sign up for one of the above at the next test date.

Sources of Test Materials

SAT   *Scholastic Aptitude Test and Achievement Tests*
College Entrance Examination Board
475 Riverside Avenue, New York, New York 10027
Also: 1947 Center Street, Berkeley, California

ACT   *American College Testing Program* (ACT), *Inc.*
ACT Division of Publications and Public Information
P. O. Box 168
Iowa City, Iowa 52240

SCAT   School and College Ability Tests
Cooperative Test Division
Education Testing Service
Princeton, New Jersey or Los Angeles, California

Otis Quick Scoring Mental Ability Test
World Book Company
Yonkers-on-Hudson, New York and Chicago, Illinois

The Henmon-Nelson Tests of Mental Ability, Revised Edition
Houghton Mifflin Company
Boston, Massachusetts

Strong Vocational Interest Blanks
Testscor, Inc.
2312 Snelling Avenue
Minneapolis, Minnesota 55404

Kuder Occupational Interest Survey
Science Research Associates, Inc.
259 Erie Street
Chicago, Illinois 60611

Study of Values by Allport, Vernon, and Lindzey
Houghton Mifflin Company
Boston, Massachusetts

Minnesota Paper Board Form
Psychological Corporation
304 East 45th Street
New York, New York 10017

Bennett Mechanical Comprehension Test
Psychological Corporation
304 East 45th Street
New York, New York 10017

GATB *General Aptitude Test Battery*
U. S. Department of Labor
Bureau of Employment Security
Washington, D. C.

CPI *California Psychological Inventory*
Consulting Psychological Press
577 College Avenue
Palo Alto, California 94306

2. When all the tests have been scored, confer with your counselor to study the results and their interpretation.

3. Discuss with members of the class your reactions to the test results.

4. To comprehend the relevancy of testing, read *Pygmalion in the Classroom* by Robert Rosenthal and Lenore Jacobson (New York: Holt, Rinehart & Winston, Inc., 1968) and *The Tyranny of Testing* by Banesh Hoffman (New York: Colliers Books, 1964).

References

1. William H. Bayer and Paul Walsh, "Are Children Born Unequal?" *Saturday Review*, October 19, 1968, p. 61ff.

2. Robert Rosenthal and Lenore Jacobson, *Pygmalion in the Classroom* (New York: Holt, Rinehart & Winston Inc., 1968). Janet D. Elashoff and Richard E. Snow, *Pygmalion Reconsidered* (Worthington, Ohio: Charles A. Jones Publishing Company, 1971).

3. Stalnaker quoted by Max Baer and Edward Roeber, *Occupational Information*, 3rd edition (Chicago: Science Research Associates, Inc., 1964), p. 196.

4. Edward K. Strong, Jr., *Vocational Interests 18 Years After College* (Minneapolis: University of Minnesota Press, 1955).

5. Reprinted with permission of the publisher from: Edward K. Strong, Jr. *Manual for Strong Vocational Interest Blanks for Men and Women*, rev. by David P. Campbell (Stanford, Cal.: Stanford University Press, 1966), p. 11.

6. American Medical Association, *Horizons Unlimited* (Chicago: The Association, 1966), p. iii.

7. Strong, *Vocational Interests*, p. 145.

8. Banesh Hoffman, *The Tyranny of Testing* (New York: Collier Books, 1964), p. 216.

8

What Experiences Can Tell You

The British poet Stephen Spender, telling about his desire to be a naturalist, described in poetic language his youthful dream of the future. Asked what made him change his mind, Spender replied, "A course in botany." (1)

....

"Accounts" to People   A business major took his first job after graduation with a prominent company as an accountant. Several months later his sister went to a vocational counselor for advice because her brother had become depressed and unhappy when he discovered that, after years spent in obtaining his degree, he disliked his work. Fortunately for him a change to the field of sales was possible.

Testing revealed that, although business was his best field, contact with people was important to him, but even before the tests were completed, the young man had left the job of accounting and obtained a job in sales.

....

What works? What works for you? What doesn't work? All theories, ideas, judgments are put to the test in experience. Moreover, experience can be the teacher and the evaluator as well.

Courses as Experience

Exploratory courses offer an opportunity to survey a field of work. Such courses as Introduction to Electronics, Principles of Data Processing, Principles of Sales, and Introduction to Law Enforcement not only present a detailed survey of specific fields but also help you to determine your ability to comprehend and perform the necessary work.

Students who change majors during college often do so as a result of realizing what specific fields are like. The undergraduates who changed from social science majors to education majors did so when they realized that the social science major was primarily an intellectual approach to a study of human relations rather than a service approach.

In the field of data processing it is important to realize the difference between machine operations (requiring craftsman-like abilities), and computer programming (requiring logical reasoning). In the field of electronics, there is a specialized area called vacuum technology which is the principle behind all space exploration. Majors need a creative, research type of mind for experimenting in this expanding work. Exploratory courses give you a working knowledge of a career field which can enable you to test your own understanding and preferences.

Prerequisite courses test your interest and ability in basic course work. Concentrated study in higher mathematics is necessary to become an engineer so that if you are considering engineering, you must analyze your proficiency in math theories. If you find chemistry distasteful, you may decide that medicine isn't for you. If you discover, however, that you are making the highest grades in a class or are finding the content highly interesting, you may wish to explore further with more advanced courses. To a certain extent any course in which you make a grade above average should be examined, since students seem tempted to devalue their best work, perhaps because it comes naturally or because it is so interesting it doesn't seem like work.

Some careers require eye and hand coordination, finger dexterity or complete manual dexterity. Such careers include a variety of skills such as pipefitting, handling earth moving equipment, airplane piloting, and dentistry. Tests for determining necessary dexterity and motor skills are mandatory for those choosing these occupations or similar ones. From your personal experience you should be able to judge to some extent your performance in the area of motor skills compared to your colleagues. If you realize that you have extraordinary dexterity and coordination, capitalize upon this by exploring various careers requiring such potential that may be open to you.

In analyzing your abilities, it is important to be honest, a difficult task if you have tentatively chosen a career. You may say, "I know I can do it if I try." Or, "I never studied in high school; that is my problem." This may or may not be the truth. There is always the counter question, "Why haven't you tried? Is there too little interest to sustain effort?" There may be perfectly acceptable reasons for not having done well in courses but you must succeed in certain courses in order to prepare for specific careers.

One-half of entering freshmen change their career preferences before they are seniors. So if a change is necessary, accept the fact with the knowledge that finding the right career can be an exciting undertaking. Fortunately, the first two years of a college curriculum usually are made up of general education courses, making it possible for a student to attempt art courses, business courses, or any others in order to find a preference without loss of credits.

A skillful instructor of geography in a small college has been responsible for a relatively large number of students who transferred to the university with a major in geography. His courses enabled the students to learn what a geographer does and to catch the excitement and worth of this profession.

On-the-Job Experience

The average young person growing up today can profit from almost any job he can get. You can learn what you like and what you dislike, what you can do and what you cannot do, and what you prefer. You will also learn about people.

Some occupations require practical experience as part of the training. When such experience comes early in the program, it helps you decide whether or not you can cope with the situation. The director of a nursing school explained that during the first semester of the program when students begin hospital training, they become aware of their suitability or unsuitability for this career. She explained further that the crucial test is handling the patient, when the prospective nurse must feel the flesh of another human being without wishing to withdraw. Here many persons fail in actual experience.

Increasing numbers of colleges provide on-the-job training for such occupations as medical assistants, dental assistants, secretaries, and X-ray technicians. If this experience comes late in the program, time may be lost when you find out a change of career is necessary. For example, doctors and teachers must serve an internship period provided at the end of training. It is important, therefore, that you have the opportunity to "sample" several kinds of work, because there are jobs that can help you test your preferences and your abilities.

The woman who works as a nurse's aide can test her preference for nursing; working in a drug store can test her knowledge of a career in pharmacy. Working as a recreation leader in a city park system or as a counselor or leader in Boy Scout camp or as a lifeguard at a swimming pool can test a young man's preference for working with young people and even for a career in sports.

....

Sandra's Exploratory Job   Sandra was a freshman in college, a declared English major, but, frankly, she disliked school and her grades were poor. In high school she had been a cheerleader, vice-president of the senior class and president of the Girls' Athletic Association and she missed such activity in college. Sandra talked with her counselor about changing to a two year college program. Because of her scores on specific tests, relatively high in art and high in sales, as well as her past effectiveness with others, the counselor suggested that she try selling during the holidays that were approaching. After contacting the business department of the college which maintained liaison with many stores in the city, Sandra obtained a job for the holidays selling in a leading sportswear shop. Her success was apparent. She reported with enthusiasm that she had been asked to continue working as a permanent employee and was going to do so on a part-time basis.

....

One large city with an outstanding program for juvenile delinquents employs suitable young men with two years of college work as counselors. Several young men with interests in penalogy or social science as a career have worked their way through college while employed at Juvenile Hall, testing their aptitude and continuing interest by actual experience.

There are many jobs, if you will search for them, that will enable you to test career choices. It may take imagination and investigation as well as persistence, but the experience will be worth it in helping make an occupational choice. There are also other advantages to working in different jobs.

Many young people work at a summer job because they need to save money for college or to help the family financially. One insight to be gained is how important money is to you. One young man astonished his classmates by saying that he had earned several thousands of dollars that summer working in a steel mill. "But I wouldn't do it again for twice that amount," he said. "Life isn't worth it."

You may take a job because you wish to feel independent, suddenly aware that assuming responsibility for a job is a mark of maturity. Taking a job away from your family and community may strengthen your independence and self-reliance. The Peace Corps and VISTA have offered this opportunity, and the National Park Service employs hundreds of young people every summer.

An important result of getting a job, almost any job, is that you will acquire experience in working with others. Since it is a truism that more persons are discharged from their work because they cannot get along with the other workers than for any other reason, you can gain the opportunity to learn about people and to learn what others expect of you.

....

Peter Drucker: A Doer   Peter Drucker said, "Here I am 58 and I still don't know what I am going to do when I grow up." Drucker is a doer, not a contemplator, and, for him, knowledge exists in action. He has had so many exciting jobs and he sees the possibility of so many more exciting jobs that he doesn't want to make any career choice final.

He continues, "My children and their respective spouses think I'm kidding when I say that, but I am not.... Life is not that categorized.... There is no way of finding out what you want to do but trying.... A job is your opportunity to find out.... Be ruthless about finding out.... You can always quit."

His advice to young people is this, "No matter what a job is, it ain't final. The first few years are trials. The probability that the first choice you make is right for you is roughly one in a million. If you decide your first choice is the right one, chances are you are just plain lazy. People believe that if they take a job for General Electric or New York University or *Psychology Today* that they have taken their vows, that the world will come to an end if it doesn't work out."

Drucker has practiced what he expounds. After he finished secondary school he went to work as an apprentice clerk in a woolen export house. After a move into investment banking in Germany, he became a newspaper man. "Until age 30," he confesses, "I was really a drifter. I know perfectly well all the things I didn't want to do with myself."

But Drucker had talent as a writer. "I am not a scholar, I am a writer," he says, "but I am not good enough to write novels." And as he continued with his experience in many jobs—as economist, professor of politics, and consultant in business management, he also continued to write. Three of his books are basic for students of the business world, *The Effective Executive*, *Managing for Results*, and *The Practice of Management*. So, actually, all of his jobs became the source of material for his finest contribution, his books. (2)

For Exploration and Discussion

1. What exploratory courses have you taken or are now taking? What have you learned? What courses for exploration would you enroll in next semester?

2. What have you learned about yourself and about work from the jobs you have held up to the present? Share this learning with the members of your class.

3. Plan for other work experiences you should have.
   a. Regularly read the Want Ads in the newspaper.
   b. Visit nearby youth employment centers.
   c. Make application to the State Employment Office or to your own College Placement Center.
   d. Discuss possible jobs with members of the class, your friends, and near-by organizations.
   e. Watch billboards for Help Wanted placards.
   f. Apply for work at businesses with which you trade.

4. With other members of the class, visit local industries, government offices, and recreation centers. Investigate, first hand, the kinds of work available in your area. Divide the sections of the city to be covered; make appointments first; and go in groups of two and three. Report your impressions to the class so that all information may be pooled for the common good.

5. Through the assistance of the librarian, locate the publications of the Department of Labor that cover employment in your district and read them continually.

6. Keep yourself open to experience by hearing speakers on specific careers, viewing career films, listening to tapes, reading current literature on expanding fields, and being alert to all work situations and possibilities. At the beginning of class sessions, comment on any unique or outstanding career opportunity you have uncovered.

7. There are several good books on how to apply for a job which may help you to do so successfully. In your library you may find these books:
   Allan Rood, *Job Strategy* (New York: McGraw Hill Book Company, 1961).
   Austin Marshall, *How to Get a Better Job* (New York: Appleton Century, 1964).
   J. I. Biegleisen, *How to Go About Getting a Job with a Future* (New York: Grosset & Dunlap, 1967).
   Henry Koch, *Jobs and How to Get Them* (San Francisco: Ken Publishing Company, 1970).

References

1. *Kuder Occupational Interest General Manual* (Chicago: Science Research Associates, Inc., 1966), p. 2.

2. Mary Harrington Hall, "A Conversation with Peter Drucker" *Psychology Today*, March 1968, pp. 21-23.

9

Your Self-Assessment

To Aristotle's advice, "Know thyself," Thomas Carlyle added, "Know thy work; too long has thy poor self deluded thee." In one sense, none of us can ever completely know himself; yet self-knowledge is basic to adjustment in the world of work or to any other part of our world.

Certain things you can know about yourself and already do know. You know your physical characteristics and your temperament, some of your talents and general abilities. But are you aware of your life style? Your personal style? Your motivations? Knowing these will enable you to discriminate more carefully when choosing the work appropriate for you.

Life Style

By *life style*, we mean the manner in which you characteristically react to your environment. To understand your life style you need to answer such questions as these:

1. When do you do your best work?
   Morning? Evening? Anytime?
   Do you think best early in the morning?
   Do you do your clearest thinking consistently in the

evening? (One young man after careful scrutiny selected as possible careers only those which would allow
him to arise late.)

2. In what physical environment are you happiest?
Outdoors? In the city?
When it is quiet? Noisy?
Well organized? Loosely organized?
With people? By yourself?
In large, luxurious surroundings? In small, friendly
surroundings?

3. What working conditions do you enjoy?
Under pressure? Without pressure?
Creative? Routine?
Giving direction? Taking direction?
Self-employed? An employee?
With a prestige company? With a small organization?

4. What kind of doer are you?
Fast? Slow?
Meticulous? Casual?
Rigid? Flexible?
Conformist? Non-conformist?
Disciplined? Careless?

5. What kind of thinker are you?
Analytical? Perceptive?
Objective? Subjective?
Scientific? Intuitive?
Do you remember best what you hear? Or see? Or
touch?
Are you a reader, a listener, or a talker? Or all of
these?

6. What kind of people do you enjoy?
A few close friends? Many friends?
Children? Old people? Sick people?
Animals?

7. What causes you frustration, anger, unhappiness?
What causes you joy, peace, contentment?

Some of these questions you may not be able to answer
at this time. But to answer honestly those you can will enable

you to realize your own preferences and unique needs for your daily activities.

Personal Orientation

Closely related to life style is personal orientation. By *personal orientation* we mean the pattern formed by certain dominant personal traits which becomes a consistent way of relating to life situations. Psychologist John P. Holland describes six different orientations:

1. The *Realistic* (Motoric) orientation is characterized by aggressive behavior, interest in activities requiring motor coordination, skill and physical strength, and masculinity. People oriented toward this role prefer "acting out" problems; they avoid tasks involving interpersonal and verbal skills and seek concrete rather than abstract problem situations.

2. The *Intellectual* (Intellectual) person's main characteristics are thinking rather than acting, organizing and understanding rather than dominating or persuading, and associability rather than sociability. These people prefer to avoid close interpersonal contact, though the quality of their avoidance seems different from their Realistic colleagues.

3. The *Social* (Supportive) people seem to satisfy their need for attention in a teaching or therapeutic situation. In sharp contrast to the Intellectual and Realistic people, Social people seek close interpersonal situations and are skilled in their interpersonal relations, while they avoid situations where they might be required to engage in intellectual problem-solving or use extensive physical skills.

4. The *Conventional* (Conforming) style is typified by a great concern for rules and regulations, great self control, subordination of personal needs, and strong identification with power and status. This kind of person prefers structure and order and thus seeks interpersonal and work situations where structure is readily available.

5. The *Enterprising* (Persuasive) people are verbally skilled, but rather than use this verbal skill to support others as the Social types do, they use it for manipulating people. They are concerned about power and status, as are

Table 7 Classification of Work to Each of Six Personal Orientations

Orientation	Types of Work	Relevant Major
Realistic	Technical and skilled trades. Working with things.	agriculture, agricultural education, physical education, recreation, industrial arts, engineering, forestry, trade, and industry
Intellectual	Scientific occupations. Working with ideas or data.	architecture, biological sciences, geography, medical technology, pharmacy, mathematics, philosophy, physical sciences, anthropology
Social	Teaching and helping occupation. Working with people.	health education, education of exceptional children and mentally retarded, speech correction, education (unclassified), nursing, occupational therapy, physical therapy, social science (general), American civilization, sociology, social work
Conventional	Clerical occupations. Working with data.	accounting, secretarial, business and commercial (general and unclassified), business education, library science, economics
Enterprising	Supervising and sales occupations. Working with people and things.	hotel and restaurant administration, hospital administration, history, international relations, political science, foreign service, industrial relations, public administration
Artistic	Artistic, musical, and literary occupations. Working with data and things.	art education, music education, English and journalism, fine and applied arts (all fields), foreign language and literature (all fields)

Based on data from John L. Holland and Robert S. Nichols, "Exploration of a Theory of Vocational Choice: A Longitudinal Study of Change in Major Field of Study," *Personnel and Guidance Journal* (November, 1964), p. 236.

the Conventional people, but differ in that they aspire to the power and status while the Conventional honor others for it.

6. The *Artistic* (Esthetic) orientation manifests strong self-expression and relations with other people indirectly through their artistic expression. Such people dislike structure, rather prefer tasks emphasizing physical skills or interpersonal interactions. They are introspective and asocial much like the Intellectuals, but differ in that they are more feminine than masculine, are impulsive, and express emotions more readily than most people. (1)

If two or more orientations in your personal style are the same or nearly the same relative strength, you will probably vacillate in your selection of an occupation; one day you may choose one environment and the next day a different one. If circumstances prevent your choosing your first clear-cut orientation, then you will probably choose an occupation appropriate to your second-strongest orientation.

Using this orientation structure, several studies have been made of its value for students, relating orientation to types of work and to college majors. See Table 7 on page 85. (2)

Within each orientation can be identified an occupational hierarchy dependent upon differences of ability, training, and motivation. For example, in the Realistic orientation one could list jobs from a high level to lower levels: architect, civil engineer, mechanic, factory worker. In the Enterprising class one might rank city manager, stockbroker, and door-to-door salesman. Among the workers of the Artistic class the hierarchy could be: concert pianist, writer, actor, photographer, and newspaper reporter.

Activity Preference

In addition to an understanding of your life style and your personal orientation, a careful analysis of your activity preference will help you select your most suitable career. By *activity preference* is meant the natural or innate preferences you may have toward involvement in job activities.

Three basic elements of involvement in any job as identified by the *Dictionary of Occupational Titles* (DOT, 1965) are data (facts, ideas, statistics), people, and things. Your degree of preference for any or all of these elements is considered a basic framework not only for vocational interests, but for your individual style of behavior as well. The DOT lists 114 worker-trait groups and assigns to them the level of involvement in these three characteristics.

One study which helps us understand the relationship of activity preference to specific jobs was done by D'Costa and Winefordner, who used information from the DOT to develop their *Cubistic Model of Vocational Interests.** The word *cubistic* here refers to the three-dimensional relationship of work to data, people, and things. The study first identified five elements for classifying work and determined the amount of involvement with data, people, and things for each classification. Then the 114 DOT worker-trait groups were divided into 24 homogeneous clusters. By testing their materials on successful and satisfied vocational education students, D'Costa and Winefordner concluded that people satisfactorily engaged in specific occupations have predictable ways of behaving. (3)

The formula used by D'Costa and Winefordner for correlating traits and worker activity is based on low, average, or high amount of involvement:

Work Classification:	Job Activity Involvement with:		
	Data	People	Things
Things and Machines	All levels	None	High
Communication of Ideas to People	High	All levels	Little or none
Efficiency and Systems	Mostly high	Average	Average
Medical Care	All levels	High	All levels
Customer Service	Low to average	Low to average	Low to average

*Material in the D'Costa and Winefordner study in this section is paraphrased and reprinted from *Ohio Vocational Interest Survey*, copyright 1970, by Harcourt Brace Jovanovich, Inc. Reprinted by special permission of the publisher.

D'Costa and Winefordner's 24 clusters, showing the attitudinal relationships toward data, people, and things and also their five work classifications, are listed below. The word "high" here means a strong, positive attitude:

Work	*Attitude*
1. Manual laborer	High on things
2. Mechanical work	High on things
3. Personal service	High on Customer Service and average on Communication of Ideas to people
4. Care of people and animals	Average on Communication of Ideas to People, on Customer Service and on Medical Care
5. Clerical	High on Customer Service and average on Efficiency and Systems and on Medical Care
6. Inspecting, sorting, testing	High on things, average on Efficiency and Systems
7. Crafts	High on things
8. Business Service	High on Customer Service
9. Nursing	High on Medical Care
10. Demonstration & Training	Above average on Communication of Ideas to People; average on Customer Service .
11. Aesthetic, Creative	High on Communication of Ideas to People
12. Theoretical Research	Above average in Efficiency & Systems
13. Business Accounting	High in Efficiency & Systems
14. Technical Appraisal	High on Things and Machines. Above average in Efficiency & Systems
15. Agriculture	High on Things and Machines

16. Engineering	High on Things and Machines; average in Efficiency & Systems
17. Communication Promotion	High in Efficiency & Systems; above average on Communication of Ideas to People
18. Managerial	High in Efficiency & Systems
19. Artistic Decoration	High on Communication of Ideas to People; average on Customer Service
20. Sales Representative	High in Efficiency & Systems average on Customer Service
21. Entertainment	High in Communication of Ideas to People
22. Education	High in Communication of Ideas to People; average in Efficiency & Systems
23. Supervision and Training	High in Efficiency & Systems
24. Medical	High in Medical Care

Anne Roe, an authority on the psychology of occupations, has developed another method of relating personal preferences to involvement in the world of work. She organizes work into two dimensions: 1) by the primary focus of the activity, and 2) by the level of responsibility and training inherent within the job. (4) The following eight categories represent Roe's grouping of workers by specific primary activities:

> I. Service: Occupations serving and attending to the personal tastes, needs, and welfare of other persons, including guidance, social work, and domestic and protective services.

> II. Business Contact: Occupations primarily concerned with the face-to-face sale of commodities, investments, real estate, and services, including demonstrator, auctioneer, and other kinds of agents where personal persuasion and the person-to-person relation is important.

III. Organization: Managerial and white collar jobs in business, industry, and government primarily concerned with the organization and efficient functioning of commercial enterprises and government activities.

IV. Technology: Occupations concerned with the production, maintenance, and transportation of commodities and utilities, including engineering, crafts (including repair work) and the machine trades, as well as transportation and communication.

V. Outdoors: Agricultural, fishing, forestry, mining and kindred occupations primarily concerned with the cultivation and preservation of crops, marine and inland water resources, mineral resources, forest products, and animal husbandry.

VI. Science: Occupations concerned primarily with scientific theory and its application other than technology.

VII. General Cultural: Occupations involved in the presentation and transmission of the general cultural heritage, including occupations in education, journalism, law, the ministry, and linguistics.

VIII. Arts and Entertainment: Occupations demanding special skills in the creative arts and in the field of entertainment, including creators and performers.

Roe's second dimension is a carefully structured classification based upon degrees of responsibility, capacity, and skill in representative occupations. In some areas the level of education overlaps, so that in certain instances either a two-year or a four-year college education may be required. Also, the same title may be assigned to different levels, depending on the duties within the title.

Level 1. At this level are the professional and managerial positions which demand independent responsibility. Here are the innovators, creators, top managers and administrators. They make policy.

When education is relevant, it is at the doctoral level or the equivalent.

Level 2. The distinction between this level and Level 1 is primarily one of degree. Independence is necessary but with narrower or less significant responsibilities both for self and others. The work is less important and has less variety of tasks. Education is at or above the bachelor level, but below the doctorate or its equivalent.

Level 3. This work could be labeled as semi-professional or small business. There is a low-level responsibility for others. It calls for the application of policy and the determination for self only (as in managing a small business). Education is at the Associate-in-Arts degree or its equivalent.

Level 4. At this level are the skilled occupations requiring apprenticeship or other special training or experience.

For the basis of her organization, Roe used many broad studies, compiling scientific evidence for the placing of specific occupations within their respective groupings. Occupational groups in Table 8 can be considered representative; corresponding or similar occupations could be given the same placement (see pages 92-93).

Motivation

In addition to life style, personal style, and activity preference, a personality factor influencing your choice of work is motivation. Motivation, different from a value system, is often subconscious, derives from a strong desire, has a definite goal, and an expectancy of success. (5)

Motivation may lead an individual into inappropriate choice. The individual who is motivated to please someone else above every other consideration may choose a career that meets the needs of another. Motivated to punish or to surpass

Table 8* Two-Way Classification of Occupations

LEVEL	I. SERVICE	II. BUSINESS CONTACT	III. ORGANIZATION	IV. TECHNOLOGY
1	Personal therapists Social work supervisors Counselors, psychological	Promoters—big business	U. S. President and Cabinet officers Industrial tycoons International bankers and merchants	Inventive geniuses Designers: auto, tools Consulting or chief engineers: architectural, civil, mechanical Ship commanders Applied scientists, consulting, chief
2	Social workers Occupational therapists Probation, truant officers, FBI agents Vocational counselors Educational counselors	Public relations men Promoters—small business	Executive, average Certified public accountants Politicians Business and government executives Officers on ships and in armed services Union officials Brokers, Bankers Buyers (large businesses)	Applied scientists, geological, chemical Factory managers Ships' technical officers Engineers: civil, architectural
3	Welfare workers—municipal YMCA, YWCA workers Employment interviewers Police sergeants Sheriffs City inspectors Sergeants—armed services	Retail and wholesale dealers Salesmen: auto, bond, real estate, insurance Confidence men	Accountants Appraisers Bank tellers Buyers (small businesses) Credit managers Draftsmen Employment managers Executives Hotel managers Small manufacturers Small business owners Postmasters; private secretaries Salesmen: specialty, technical Statisticians	Aviators Contractors: building, carpentry, plumbing Draftsmen, engineers Engineers: marine, chief Factory foremen Radio operators Small factory managers
4	Barbers Chefs Hairdressers Headwaiters Lifeguards Practical nurses Policemen Religious workers Stewards	Auctioneers Buyers House canvassers and agents Interviewers, polls	Agents, freight Bookkeepers, Cashiers Clerks: credit, mail Dispatchers Floorwalkers Foremen, warehouse Inspectors, telephone and telegraph Sales clerks Station agents Stenographers Inspectors	Craftsmen of every kind: Jewelers Bricklayers Printers Glass-blowers Blacksmiths Machinists Plumbers Electricians Cabinet makers Mechanics: auto, plane

LEVEL	V. OUTDOOR	VI. SCIENCE	VII. GENERAL CULTURE	VIII. ART & ENTERTAINMENT
1	Consulting specialists	Independent research scientist, all fields Mathematician Medical specialist, all types Museum curator University and college faculty in science	Editors (e.g. *New York Times*) Educational administrators Clergymen, high ranking Judge, federal Justice, U.S. Supreme Court Lawyer, high ranking Scholars, university faculty	Creative artists: poet, sculptor, writer; composer, choreographer Museum curator, fine arts Performers, at highest level: actor, singer, dancer, concert artist, conductor, director, athletic champion Teacher, at highest level
2	Applied scientists, agronomists, etc. Horticulturists Landowners and operators, large Landscape architects Range management specialists Wildlife specialists	Dentist Nurse Pharmacist Scientist, semi-independent Veterinarian	Clergyman, priest Columnist Educational administrator Editor, average News commentator Teacher, high school and elementary	Athlete, professional Athletic coach Art critic Circus performer Designers, stage and jewelry Music arranger, orchestral Performers, average Teachers, lower level
3	Beekeeper County agents Farmers, individual owner Fish culturists Horticulturist Forest ranger Lumber camp manager Nurseryman (owner) Poultryman Tree surgeon Truck gardener Surveyor	Chiropodist Chiropractor Laboratory technician Medical technician Weather observer X-ray technician	Judge, municipal Justice of Peace Law clerk Librarian Radio announcer Reporter	Advertising writer Designer: clothes, textiles, rugs, etc. Interior decorator Music arranger, popular Showman Stage designer, average Vaudeville performer
4	Fisherman (owner) Laboratory tester, dairy products Landscape gardener Miner Oil well driller Ore grader Shaftman	Embalmer Technical assistants		Advertising artist Decorator, window drapes Illustrator Racing car driver Monument maker

*Reprinted from: Anne Roe, *The Psychology of Occupations* (New York: John Wiley and Sons, Inc., 1959), p. 151, by special permission of the publishers.

another, the individual may also choose unwisely. A commitment to another person or to a cause may result in an unusual or perhaps only tolerable choice of work.

Achievement motivation, however, affects nearly everyone. (6) This motivation, even when risk is involved, may be a desire to master the environment or else a strong desire to avoid failure. People who fear failure avoid competitive behavior and aim too high or too low. They avoid accurate information concerning their abilities and their suitability for a chosen occupation, or considering information which involves high achievement; frequently they will set defensively high or low goals so there is little risk of failure. On one hand, a bright young man who decides not to go to college may be trying to avoid career situations where some risk of failure might exist. On the other hand, there is little risk of failure involved for the young girl who plans to become a movie star because she is so unlikely to attain her goal that there will be no personal sense of failure if she fails. Because of the effect on the individual's future, a scrutiny of his achievement motivation might result in a better vocational choice.

The individual with a strong motivation to achieve is the one who is able to find the greatest satisfaction from his work. One study repeated sixteen times in a wide variety of occupations ranging from scientists to household help in Finland, Hungary, and the Soviet Union, as well as the United States, confirmed the significance of the achievement motivation. (7) Few studies in industrial psychology have been repeated so often with such overwhelming results as this: that personal satisfaction in work comes from a sense of achievement.

Motivation cannot be bought. A motivated man will do things of his own volition that will exceed what he could be made to do by offers of other rewards.

Some persons have a tendency to respond in a particular manner regardless of the circumstances. Osipow quotes Heath, who analyzed student behavior in regard to vocational activity and concluded that four styles exist: the "reasonable adventurer," involved in life and full of zest and tolerance; the "non-committed," showing a fearful noninvolvement with life; the "hustler," upward striving and busy defending himself against threats to his striving; and the "plunger," whose behavior reflects a fearful impulsiveness. (8)

"To Be that Self Which One Truly Is"

Personality is still much of a mystery to psychologists and consequently cannot be the only basis for career choice. Yet no successful career decision can be made without the consideration of individual differences. The worker is first of all a person, and must strive "to be that self which he truly is."

In regard to work, you must ask of yourself:

1. What type of activity do I like best? Working with people? Things? Ideas? Or any combination of these?

2. In what setting do I prefer to work? In an office? Outdoors? Under pressure?

3. In what kind of organization am I interested? Government? Academic? Medical? Industrial? (A specific industry?) Business? (A specific business?)

4. What do I wish to achieve? Why do I wish to achieve it? How much do I want to achieve it?

The next chapter will discuss your personal needs.

For Exploration and Discussion

1. The important exploration, here, is an inner scrutiny.
   a. Determine your life style
   b. Determine your personal style
   As you analyze yourself, confer with your counselor and close friends for their reactions.

2. Some of the obstacles to facing oneself honestly have been described by a leading social psychologist. For further research into this sensitive subject, read *Man for Himself* by Erich Fromm (New York: Holt, Rinehart & Winston, Inc., 1947) and *Escape from Freedom* by Erich Fromm (New York: Holt, Rinehart & Winston, Inc., 1941).

3. Can you find where you belong among Holland's six orientations? Is one orientation clearly dominant? Are two or more orientations of the same or nearly the same strength? Establish a hierarchy for yourself of each of the orientations, placing at the bottom the one most unlike you. Number it 6. Then, build until you come to the one most like you, number 1.

4. You can develop your own hierarchy within each class. At which level are you aiming? At which level should you be aiming?

5. To learn more about the kinds of work that would be classified in any one of D'Costa and Winefordner's 24 clusters, refer to the 3rd edition, Volume II of the *Dictionary of Occupational Titles*, pages 217ff, usually filed at the library reference desk.

References

1. Samuel H. Osipow, *Theories of Career Development* (New York: Appleton-Century-Crofts, 1968), pp. 40-41.

2. John L. Holland and Robert S. Nichols, "Exploration of a Theory of Vocational Choice: A Longitudinal Study of Change in Major Field of Study," *Personnel & Guidance Journal*, November 1964, p. 236.

3. Ayres D'Costa and David W. Winefordner, "The Cubistic Model of Vocational Interests." Paper presented at the American Educational Research Association Convention, Chicago, February 8-10, 1968.

4. Material on this study paraphrased from: Anne Roe, *The Psychology of Occupations* (New York: John Wiley & Son, Inc., 1956), pp. 151 ff.

5. Osipow, *Theories of Career Development*, p. 162.

6. Osipow, *Theories of Career Development*, pp. 162-165.

7. Frederick Herzberg, "Motivation, Money and Morale," *Psychology Today*, Vol. 1, No. 10, March 1968, p. 66.

8. Osipow, *Theories of Career Development*, p. 167.

10

Your Personal
Needs

In the process of growing up, each person, according to his role in the family, is influenced by a different environment. This fact, in addition to the unlikely chance of having identical genes, accounts for the uniqueness of each individual.

It may be that you are critical of your upbringing, believing you would not have some of your problems and some of your traits if you had been raised differently. You may be right. However, no one has a perfect home environment, just as no one is perfect.

It is when we are able to take responsibility for ourselves, to accept what we are, with our strengths and our weaknesses that we can change what is within our power to change; we must do the best we can with what is. Your personality needs and your character needs are probably the result of the way you were reared, plus your reaction to this upbringing.

Personality Needs

Psychologists have known for many years that persons with certain personal needs seem to choose certain careers. Within this concept Siegman and Peck made a series of studies about the underlying need patterns that exist within various vocational groups. These studies were based on these beliefs: first, that people have specific personality need patterns; second, that vocations differ in their job-role requirements; third, that people choose vocations because they believe, consciously or unconsciously, that the job-role requirements of the field they select allow them to satisfy dominant personality needs; fourth, that the job-role requirements of a vocation best satisfy the dominant personality needs of a certain kind of individual; and finally, that most people in a vocation share a common need pattern which differs from the need pattern characteristic of people in other vocational areas. (1)

What are the most common personality needs? Human personality needs have been classified by a test called the Adjustive Check List (ACL) in this manner:

Dominance	a need to lead and persuade others
Affiliation	a need to seek and sustain numerous personal friendships
Heterosexuality	the need to derive emotional satisfaction from the opposite sex
Action	a need for action, practical or ideal
Achievement	a need to accomplish
Nurturance	a need to help others
Succorance	a need to sustain others
Endurance	a need to endure
Deference	a need to look to others for direction
Order	a need to have order
Abasement	a need for support
Social	a need for social approval (2)

The need for Dominance is strong in persons of the Conventional or Enterprising type and is a low need for persons in the Realistic, Intellectual, or Artistic type (see Chapter 9). In addition to Dominance, the most differentiating personality needs were Affiliation and Heterosexuality, which were of less than average importance to the Realistic and Artistic types and were of more than average importance to the Conventional and Enterprising types.

The value to you of knowing the personality needs of various workers is not that you scrutinize yourself to see if you are the same shape peg for the same shape hole, but rather to enable you to be aware of the need fulfillments that can be found in various kinds of work.

You may or may not be aware of having any personality needs. In his theory of career choice, Holland emphasizes that adequacy of occupational choice is largely a function of the adequacy of self-knowledge and occupational knowledge. (3) The greater the amount and accuracy of information the individual has about himself in relation to job possibilities the more adequate is his choice.

Character Needs

In the process of growing up, some persons develop unusual character strengths and some, unusual weaknesses. To select astronauts, many tests were devised to determine the stability, character, and intelligence of the men forced to endure remarkable hardships. Certain work requires unusual strengths; for example, persons chosen for the Peace Corps are carefully screened. Moreover, traits of leadership, persistance, and trustworthiness are crucial in certain careers, and persons with these traits are invaluable.

In contrast, there are persons who have character weaknesses: the alcoholic, the gambler, the procrastinator, the immature individual. Persons with strong tendencies to such destructive behavior need to take this fact into consideration in choosing a career. Case histories reveal that alcoholics need careers free from pressures, persons with strong gambling tendencies need to be free from the temptation of handling large sums of money, and procrastinators need supervision. Fortunately, persons with decided weaknesses are not forced to withdraw from society, but careful planning and self-knowledge are necessary for them to make the required decisions.

Some careers seem to have built-in temptations which without proper concern may threaten marriage and family living. Some individuals need to protect themselves from such temptations. Consider the story of Johnny, the Band Leader.

....

Johnny, the Band Leader   Johnny's father was the leader of a relatively well-known dance band during the twenties and early thirties. For ten years preceding his death, Johnny's father made over $100,000 a year. However, when he died, the money from his estate barely covered the funeral expenses.

At the time of his father's death, Johnny was a freshman at a university. His ambition was to become an undertaker because in that profession he would always have work and, therefore, presumably, money. However, due to his father's death, Johnny had to drop out of the university. At the insistence of his family and friends, he agreed to take over his father's position as band director . . . .

A few years later Johnny quit the music business because his girl friend would not marry him until he did. She said she would refuse to bring up their children in the sort of life they would have to lead with a band on the road all the time. During this period Johnny worked for several oil companies but he was like "a fish out of water." In desperation, he organized another band.

But this time he decided that he would never go on the road again and although he has had many opportunities to do so, he has stuck by that decision.

Having lived with music and show business for most of his life, he knows the pitfalls involved. He knows that one can easily become disgusted with the irregular life and turn to drink or to drugs to escape. He knows too that it is hard to stay married when a husband and wife are separated for months at a time, and when temptations present themselves in varying and intriguing forms. He knows too that in order to be a success in show business, one has to sacrifice personal liberty.

In addition to continuing his band, Johnny started a theatrical booking agency because the life span of a person in that business is longer than that of a performer. No amount of persuasion from well-meaning friends and associates had been able to induce him to move the agency to either New York or Hollywood where the big money is. Johnny does not like the phoniness, the rapid pace, or the tension to be found in either city.

He has not made records because, again, he put his family first. Records demand personal sacrifice. They have to be promoted and, if they are hits, personal appearances must be made on disk jockey shows all over the country.

What has he gained by his insistence upon remaining in his home town with his small, nationally-unknown band and booking agency? He says, "I was there to put a quarter under a pillow when one of my kids lost a tooth and I will be there when they graduate from school."

Today, Johnny is a successful and satisfied head of a family and a business. He has profited by the mistakes of his father and his own experience. (4)

....

Special Needs

Persons with special needs are the disabled and the deprived.

One blind student explained to his counselor who was administering an oral test, "I may be disabled, but I'm not handicapped." This statement can be true when the disabled person approaches his career with the understanding that there is a place in the world of work that meets his special need.

Although the deprived person may not know his own need, other people are helping him to identify it and find his "place in the sun." Educational Opportunity Programs in community colleges, state colleges and universities are designed to provide economic aid in the form of work-study programs, grants, scholarships, loans, and also tutorial service for those who wish it.

Educational assistance has changed the lives of many community college students. The public community college, in most states, is an "open-door college" which means a student is welcome regardless of any test scores, academic achievement, or financial ability. Even a high school diploma is not necessary if the applicant is over eighteen. At the community college a student has the opportunity to make up his academic deficiencies and develop occupational skills in an Associate in Arts (AA) degree program such as Dental Assisting, Electronic Technology, Nursing, Merchandising, Engineering Drafting, and many others.

With the advantages of the tutorial service, disadvantaged students, as well as students who have had poor academic records in high school, are developing unsuspected potential. Jesse Ruiz reported with enthusiasm that he had been accepted at the University of California. Jesse took three semesters of remedial English before he could enroll in the regular composition course at the community college where he later made honor grades. And he is not the great exception; many students in community colleges start with remedial programs.

The plight of the deprived person is that there seems to be no work for him. In an article in *Saturday Review,* John Tebbel explained that manpower in the United States is in short supply while 3,000,000 Americans are unemployed, chiefly those who are unskilled. He states that it is our national shame that a very large part of the unemployed live in poor housing and have neither the education nor the training in a specific skill to get a job. (5)

Dropouts from high school also find themselves on the "unwanted" list. As a hopeful beginning, dropouts, persons in minority groups, and unskilled persons sometimes can enroll in special training classes, designed to help them find a successful place in the work world.

Self-Acceptance

To achieve mature adjustment, you must first recognize and accept yourself as you are, then progress toward growth, change, and fulfillment. Making believe you are different from what you are, hating yourself, striking out at others, or just ignoring the facts, will not meet your needs. Making one small move to change the situation, however, can make the difference.

Contemplate the fate of a literary friend, Miniver Cheevy, who did not try to change, but daydreamed his life away.

Miniver Cheevy

Miniver Cheevy, child of scorn
Grew lean while he assailed the seasons;

He wept that he was ever born,
  And he had reasons.

Miniver loved the days of old
  When swords were bright and steeds were prancing,
The vision of a warrior bold
  Would set him dancing.

Miniver sighed for what was not,
  And dreamed, and rested from his labors;
He dreamed of Thebes and Camelot,
  And Priam's neighbors.

Miniver mourned the ripe renown
  That made so many a name so fragrant;
He mourned Romance, now on the town
  And Art, a vagrant.

Miniver loved the Medici,
  Albeit he had never seen one:
He would have sinned incessantly
  Could he have been one.

Miniver cursed the commonplace
  And eyed a khaki suit with loathing:
He missed the medieval grace
  Of iron clothing.

Miniver scorned the gold he sought,
  But sore annoyed was he without it;
Miniver thought, and thought, and thought,
  And thought about it.

Miniver Cheevy, born too late,
  Scratched his head and kept on thinking;
Miniver coughed, and called it fate,
  And kept on drinking. (6)

A modern Miniver clutters his life with trivia, trusting his life to fate while he busily goes through superficial motions. For him, Kenneth Fearing has written "Dirge."*

Dirge

1-2-3 was the number he played but today the number came 3-2-1;
   bought his Carbide at 30 but it went to 29; had the favorite at Bowie but the track was slow —

O, executive type, would you like to drive a floating power, knee-action, silk-upholstered six? Wed a Hollywood star? Shoot the course in 58? Draw to the ace, king, jack?
O, fellow with a will who don't take no, watch out for three cigarettes on the same, single match; O democratic voter born in August under Mars, beware of liquidated rails —

Denouement to denouement, he took a personal pride in the certain, certain way he lived his own, private life, but, nevertheless, they shut off his gas; nevertheless, the bank foreclosed; nevertheless, the landlord called; nevertheless, the radio broke,

And twelve o'clock arrived just once too often, just the same he wore one gray tweed suit, bought one straw hat, drank one straight Scotch, walked one short step, took one long look, drew one deep breath, just one too many,

And wow he died as wow he lived,
   going whop to the office and blooie home to sleep and biff got married and bam had children and oof got fired, zowie did he live and zowie did he die.

Very much missed by the circulation staff of the New York Evening Post; deeply, deeply mourned by the B.M.T.,

Wham, Mr. Roosevelt; pow, Sears Roebuck; awk, big
    dipper; bop, summer rain;
bong, Mr., bong, Mr., bong, Mr., bong. (7)

As never before, individual differences are being examined and respected in our society by sociologists, psychologists, educators, and vocational counselors. New agencies are being formed and sums of money appropriated to assist in innovative ways the persons who are "dropouts" from school, disadvantaged or oppressed, physically or emotionally handicapped, and "misfits" in any way. The value of each individual and the need for him in our society are exciting assertions of the youthful revolution.

For Exploration and Discussion

1. Identify ways in which your environment is different from that of your sister or brother.

2. By thoughtful consideration, determine your personality needs; your character needs; your motivation.

3. Talk with a counselor or someone who knows you well concerning your personal needs and growth. Group therapy or group

confrontation are an effective way to comprehend and accept one's personal needs. Many colleges organize and sponsor such groups and your counselor could arrange for you to join one if you request it.

4. Studies you may wish to read which stress man's personal problems in a confused society are:

David Reisman, *The Lonely Crowd* (New Haven: Yale University Press, 1950).

Karen Horney, *The Neurotic Personality of Our Time* (New York: W. W. Norton & Company Inc., 1964).

Important studies of man's psychological development are:

Carl Rogers, *On Becoming a Person* (Boston: Houghton-Mifflin Co., 1961).

Abraham Maslow, *Motivation and Personality* (New York: Harper & Row, 1954).

Novels which stress man's critical need for wholeness are:

Franz Kafka, *The Trial* (New York: Alfred A. Knopf, 1957).

Albert Camus, *The Stranger* (New York: Alfred A. Knopf Inc., 1946).

George Orwell, *1984* (New York: The New American Library, Inc., 1954)

Oral reports on any of these books by members of the class who have read them could be the beginning of a profitable discussion.

5. Devise a perfect environment for a growing child and discuss your invention with the class.

References

1. Samuel H. Osipow, "Personality and Career," *Theories of Career Development* (New York: Appleton-Century-Crofts, 1968), pp. 180-181.

2. Martin J. Bohn, "Psychological Needs Related to Vocational Personality Types," *Journal of Counseling Psychology*, Vol. 13, No. 3, January, 1966, pp. 307-308.

3. Samuel H. Osipow, "Holland's Career Typology Theory of Vocational Behavior," *Theories of Career Development*, p. 44.

4. "Johnny, the Band Leader: A Vocational Biography," *Vocational Guidance Quarterly*, Vol. 12, No. 3, Spring 1964, pp. 194-196. Pre-

pared by graduate students at the University of Missouri under the supervision of Robert Callis, Professor of Education.

5. John Tebbel, "People and Jobs," *Saturday Review*, December 30, 1967, p. 8.

6. Edwin Arlington Robinson, "Miniver Cheevy." In *Collected Poems of Edwin Arlington Robinson* (New York: The Macmillan Company, 1927), pp. 347-48.

7. Kenneth Fearing, "Dirge." *New and Selected Poems* (Bloomington, Ind.: Indiana University Press, 1956), p. 27.

11

Getting the Facts

What should happen when you narrow your choice of career to two or three occupations? What happens when you make a tentative choice? What should you do when you discover an area of genuine interest?

It is time to take action. It is time to take three critical steps: 1) explore the vocational choice through intensive reading; 2) visit places where the work takes place; then 3) interview persons who are engaged in that work.

Research

The library is the place to go for up-to-date, accurate information on the nature of specific careers. There you will discover an abundance of authoritative, appropriate, and useful materials in occupational information files, on tapes, in books, pamphlets, magazines, and monographs. Since all the materials will not be of equal value, you must use them with discrimination. Here are some guides for your library research:

1. In viewing films or listening to tapes, realize that what you are observing is general in nature and probably somewhat glamorized.

2. Pamphlets and monographs published by industries may be attempting to induce you to try a career with

them and, consequently, will minimize the more un-
favorable aspects of the work.

3. Information must be up to date, so check the publishing date of materials you are reading.

4. Look for facts. Conclusions which reflect the opinion
of the authors may not be your conclusions.

5. Consult several sources to get a balanced viewpoint.

6. Look for information pertaining to your local area
as well as to the country as a whole. This is particularly
important if you plan to stay in your present locality.

Occupational Outlook Handbook

Not to be missed is a volume published by the Bureau of
Labor Statistics, the *Occupational Outlook Handbook*, containing a large number of monographs on various kinds of
work, grouped for convenience in this manner: "Professional
and Managerial," "Clerical," "Sales," "Service," and "Skilled
and Manual." The information on each occupation is developed
under these headings: "Nature of Work," "Where Employed,"
"Training, Qualifications and Advancement," "Employment
Outlook," and "Earnings and Working Conditions," followed
by a list of "where to go for more information." The accuracy
of this information is maintained by the Department of Labor's
thorough revision every two years. Be sure to find the current
edition.

The government is responsible for continuing research
and publication on occupations, and because of the facilities
at their service and the nature of their goals, their publications
are reliable and useful. You will probably find much of their
literature.

Dictionary of Occupational Titles

The United States Employment Service publishes the
Dictionary of Occupational Titles (DOT) with which you will

want to be familiar. The third edition, published in 1965, contains not only the definition of 22,000 different jobs (35,550 titles), but also a brief description of each occupation. Obsolete jobs in the old edition are deleted, and approximately 6,000 new jobs are added. Published in two volumes, a supplement was added in 1966 adding details to the descriptions of working conditions, physical demands, and training time. Volume I consists of job definitions that contain information of what is done, how it is done, and why it is done. The definitions are arranged alphabetically by their titles and alternate titles which are names by which the same jobs are known in various sections of the country. Volume II groups the occupations groups into two categories and includes precise details of job structure and worker traits.

In the job-structure category, all jobs are placed into groupings with other jobs having the same basic characteristics to help the user see the relationships among the various occupations. Each group is divided and subdivided to give a complete picture of job structures. There are nine such groups:

1. Professional, technical, and managerial

2. Clerical and sales

3. Service

4. Farming, fishing, forestry, and related occupations

5. Processing occupations

6. Machine trades occupations

7. Bench work occupations

8. Structural work occupations

9. Miscellaneous

In the worker-trait category, occupations are grouped with other occupations requiring the same kinds of worker traits, identifying the abilities, personal traits and individual characteristics required to achieve average success in a particular job. This part consists of 22 groups with sub-groups. The information includes appropriate aptitudes, interests, and temperament, and also establishes the physical demands of the job, the working conditions, the training required, and methods of entering the occupation.

Because these volumes are comprehensive, they are not easy to read. To find the exact information you want will take time, but it will be worth it. Besides being up to date, the DOT can help you narrow your consideration to those groups appropriate for you and will give you scope in selecting what is suitable.

Other Sources of Information

Undoubtedly there are books and pamphlets on many careers listed in the card catalogue of your library. There also may be a selected career library the librarian could point out to you.

Two good books, *A Guide to Careers Through College Majors* by J. Leonard Steinberg (1) and *Your College Degree* by Vernon H. Reeves (2), contain descriptions of fields of work, including requirements and opportunities with attention given to specialized areas. *A Guide to Careers* has an Appendix which contains an extensive listing of "Associations and Journals Related to Occupational Fields" with the proper addresses, and a listing of Civil Service and Foreign Service Opportunities. *Your College Degree* gives the course requirements for career majors and other usable information.

Periodicals

Periodicals are worthwhile because they are timely and because they often carry information on small or comparatively unknown fields of work. Any periodical published for readers employed in certain occupations could be informative in finding out more about that occupation. For a list of journals, consult your *Magazine Index File* and for magazine articles on different careers, refer to the *Readers Guide to Periodical Literature.*

Baer and Roeber provide an annotated list of periodicals that contains contemporary and specialized occupational information:

Changing Times, the Kiplinger Magazine. Contains articles on careers, training, aptitude testing, applying for jobs, and opportunities in small businesses.

Glamour Magazine. Every issue of this woman's magazine carries features on jobs for women. Job facts are often presented through case histories.

Journal of College Placement. Each issue carries articles written by specialists on occupations of special interest to college graduates.

Mademoiselle. This magazine for young women carries career charts and articles plus features about college as part of its College and Career Department.

Monthly Labor Review. Often contains reports of occupational surveys conducted by the Bureau, and every issue includes reports on wages and hours in specific industries or occupations.

Occupational Outlook Quarterly. Designed as a current supplement to the *Occupational Outlook Handbook.* It contains outlook reports on occupations and industries surveyed by the Bureau of Labor Statistics.

Seventeen. Issued monthly by Triangle Publications. This periodical for teen-aged girls frequently carries articles on specific occupations or general employment problems of interest to them.

Your Future Occupation. Published by Randall Publishing Company. Offers current information to high school students on occupations and training. (3)*

The magazine *Psychology Today*, incorporating *Careers Today*, published by Communications Research Machines, Inc., combines a vigorous, modern, youthful approach to the world of work, society's work, and psychedelic art.

*From *Occupational Information* by Max F. Baer, Ed.D. and Edward C. Roeber, Ph.D. © 1951, 1958, 1964, Science Research Associates, Inc. Reprinted by permission of the publisher.

Visitations

Reading current information on vocational literature may leave you uninformed in one important aspect of a vocation — the life style that is a part of each occupation. The third edition of the DOT has included in the job analysis a description of working conditions, and a new book, *Unabashed Career Guide* by Peter Sandman (4), captures the flavor of several specific occupations by stating both the physical and psychological characteristics of each job. These are not enough. There is something else you need to know about the work you are considering: what happens each day on the job.

Visiting the location of your potential job and observing what happens there is one way to find out about the working pattern of the job. If you are interested in being a newspaper reporter, visit the newspaper office or plant, not for one fifteen minute period, but for half a day, two or three different days. If you are interested in drafting or design, visit the drafting room of a large industry and observe what the workers are doing.

The adult world of work is generous in giving vocational information and assistance. In one instance, the chief of police in a large city permitted an inquiring student to spend the day riding with an officer in the patrol car.

A young doctor visited a careers class to give a talk on Careers in Medicine. Arriving late because of an emergency involving a child, he began his talk by relating to the class the hour-by-hour activities of his day. After class, he invited two students interested in becoming doctors to spend a day with him, beginning at 7:30 in the morning. The men accepted, and consequently learned much about the responsibilities of a young doctor, specializing in pediatrics, which they could learn in no other way.

Not knowing the working style of an occupation may cost you both suffering and loss of time. A first-year teacher resigned at the end of his first semester because of the tensions which arose daily when dealing with children and their parents. A young man was shocked to find how boring it was to be an accountant stationed at a desk. A nurse in training had to revise her career plans when she realized how repelled she was by the physical contacts that were part of her daily task. Getting a realistic understanding of what is involved in the daily routine of a career is not easy, but it is essential.

Since you may feel hesitant about visiting places of work, make an appointment first (the personnel man can probably tell you whom to contact), and take an interested friend with you. Be persistent, though not obnoxious, in finding out what you need to know.

Interviews

Talking with persons who are employed in the work that you have tentatively chosen can provide information obtainable in no other way. Seek advice from friends, instructors, or relatives about the best people to interview. Just as in visiting industries and other places of work, first call and make an appointment, only this time, go by yourself. Prepare yourself for the interview by doing intensive research on the career itself. With a proper background of information, your questions will be more relevant.

What should you ask? What do you want to know that only the worker can tell you? Here are some possible questions:

1. Why did you choose this line of work?

2. In what ways do you find your work satisfying? Dissatisfying?

3. In relationship to other jobs, what are the advantages of your work? Disadvantages?

4. What do you consider the important qualifications for this work?

5. What training or education do you consider essential?

6. What advice would you give a young person who is considering this line of work?

To get more than one point of view, try interviewing personnel men who employ workers for large companies and organizations, or talk to teachers of vocational education or of a related subject field. Relevant questions asked by a serious young person are a compliment to the worker being interviewed. In most instances, you will receive respectful, courteous answers.

Organizing the Data

Once you have collected all the information you can about your tentative choice of career, you need to organize the data to make the best possible judgments and decisions. Following are some student reports which demonstrate the results of their experiences in research and investigation.

....

A Career in Veterinary Medicine?   This report is on my investigation into the field of veterinarian medicine. It relates how I decided to explore this field, what reading I did, the persons I interviewed, and the results of my exploration; that is, how it will affect my future.

All through high school I had been interested in science, particularly biology. This is where I made my best grades. It always seemed that courses in biology were more fun than work. This feeling continued into college where I took Biology 21A and Biology 1 and received A's in both.

It is no surprise that I enjoyed these classes so much. It seems as a child I was forever carting home birds, snakes, insects, lizards — just an uncountable collection of species which, I am sure, would have prided any zoo in the world. But, I might add, much to my mother's distress.

I was not only interested in the field of Biology, but seemed to have a high aptitude for it. For example, the highest score which I received on my ACT was 30 in Natural Science. Occupational surveys which I took in Career Planning seemed to strengthen this fact. My highest scores on the Strong Vocational Interest Survey were: biologist, physician, chemist, forest service, farmer, pharmacist and physical therapist. Most of these revolve around the life sciences. My Kuder results showed high interest in Forestry (49), Animal Husbandry (46), Agriculture (46), Electrical Engineering (46) , and Veterinarian (44).

I looked at the scores and decided I didn't want to be an engineer. It was too dry and mathematical, as were chemistry and pharmacy. I didn't feel I could make enough money in forestry or agriculture; money was high on my values test. From the remaining fields I chose in order of preference: biology, physician, and veterinarian. I decided to look into the veterinarian field. This I did by interviewing two people who were well established.

The first was Dr. Calvin W. Schwabe, chairman of the Department of Veterinary Medicine of the University of California, Davis. After many letters and a lengthy wait, I finally secured an appointment with Dr. Schwabe at his office in Herring Hall. There we talked about what one must do to become a veterinarian. He told me that after I had completed 60 units (with 17 in biology, and 25 in chemistry), I could then apply in January for the next fall semester. It is possible to apply before all the requirements are met, just as long as all 60 units are completed by June before the fall semester. He said that it would probably be best for me to complete the required units at City College or a state college.

Students are accepted mainly on the basis of grades. A high GPA with no pass-fail grades in the important courses is essential. One's past experience with animals and one's moral character are also taken into consideration. He said that if I were accepted, I would have to complete a minimum of six years' study to become a veterinarian, which may actually be a harder curriculum than that required for a physician. He also estimated that it would cost me at least $2,000 a year.

Then Dr. Schwabe took me on a tour of the school. I was surprised at the fact that there is practically an entire farm right on campus where students can get firsthand experience in handling animals. They also do extensive research in the laboratory on campus. Dr. Schwabe pointed out the many directions which I could take in this field, that is, a focus on farm animals, pets, zoo animals, government work, teaching, or private practice.

The other person I interviewed was Dr. Franklin of the Acacia Pet Clinic on Almaden Expressway. At his office we talked about the pros and cons of his field, how he liked it, what mistakes he made, what advice he would give to a person going into his profession, and many other things.

Dr. Franklin works with one other veterinarian who is his partner in their clinic which cost about $100,000. The clinic nets about $100,000 a year and each partner takes home about $20,000. They have several persons working for them as janitors and receptionists. Dr. Franklin told me that private practice is a good way to go.

Dr. Franklin pointed out that a veterinarian could take long vacations, but that you can earn more if you wish by working harder. In other words, he sort of sets his own income. He also stated that he just plain likes his work.

As bad points about his work, he stated that one out of every three dollars he makes goes to the government. Also the red tape he must go through is staggering. And he really dislikes being awakened at 4 a.m. to take care of a pet who has been sick for a week and could have been brought in any time in the previous couple of days. He also stated that most of the work is routine and boring, such as vaccinations which are the "bread and butter" of the profession. As he talked, I watched him deliver two puppies which didn't seem all that boring. But maybe after one hundred times it might get tiresome.

He went on to tell me that loving animals is not that important, although he grew up around animals as he lived on a farm. This surprised me as I thought he would surely tell me that I should love animals if I wished to become a veterinarian.

He showed me all around the clinic which was surprisingly clean in spite of all the stories I had heard about dirty kennels.

It was all very exciting and overall it doesn't seem like such a bad field to go into — with the money, working conditions, and vacations. As for me, I am not sure if this is the one. I don't want to commit myself just yet although it does look mighty good. I know it would be hard getting in, but it would be worth it.

Next semester I am quitting school and joining the Merchant Marine. After that I will come back to college and then I will decide which direction I want to take.

Doug Whitman

....

Interviews with Electronics Workers   Ever since I got out of the service, I've wanted to go into electronics of some sort but I was totally unfamiliar with the field. Before entering the service I was in construction and although I made good wages, I did not like that type of work.

My mechanical scores were the highest in all of the tests and I had strong interests in electronics, so I decided to investigate the job possibilities by interviewing several people working in electronics.

Interview with William Uderitz, IBM Customer Engineering. He was very helpful in explaining just what a Customer Engineer is and what he does at IBM. He explained that one should have good mechanical skills and be at least a high school graduate with some knowledge of electronics. He showed me the test that you must take in order to become an IBM Customer Engineer. I also learned that this position starts out at approximately $450 to $500 a month with good promotional opportunities. He further explained the advantages and disadvantages of being employed by IBM.

Interview with Anthony Zeppa, San Jose City College Electronics Department. Mr. Zeppa explained the jobs in Electronics, dealing with the engineer, senior technician, field man and junior technician. Generally speaking, a person starts out in this field as a junior technician, and various opportunities and promotions occur from there. He also added that the amount of salary depended on the education and experience the individual has and the position he holds in this field.

Technicians are in demand, especially those with a college education. It was interesting to find that most students have several positions offered to them before they even start seeking employment and that a junior technician with an AA degree usually receives approximately $550 a month starting salary. Also he directed me to some of the different types of courses and told me the ones that I would have to take to complete my education in this field.

Interview with W. John Tolson, San Jose City College Vacuum Technology Department. My interview with Mr. Tolson stimulated my thinking in a totally new field. He explained what vacuum technology is and how it works. I was quite surprised to hear of the many uses of vacuum technology at present and in the near future. It is a relatively new science that is growing very rapidly with unlimited openings. He explained a new theory that used vacuum technology as the motivation of a new transportation system. This science was also used to develop the new Maxim freeze-dried coffee. He also showed me through his laboratory and explained the different instruments and machines.

The course meets four hours a day, five days a week for two semesters, followed by two semesters of electronics. With this education, an individual would make approximately the same as a junior technician — $550. As in electronics, a student in this field is offered many jobs before he even finishes his training.

Mr. Tolson was extremely helpful and gave an open invitation to any students wanting to know more about vacuum technology to visit him, which I think would be a worthwhile experience for anyone.

Interview with George Vlahakis, San Jose City College Business Data Processing Department. Through this interview I received further knowledge on programming, customer engineering, and basic operation of the computer. Mr. Vlahakis explained to me that I would have to minor in accounting with a data processing major.

He basically covered the same thing that Mr. Uderitz from IBM mentioned dealing with customer engineering.

After learning more about this field, I decided I would be better suited for a position which does not deal with the operating of computers. The customer engineering does sound interesting but I can achieve this through my electronics major. The wages were about the same as the other fields.

All in all, I'm quite satisfied with the course of study in beginning electronics I am presently taking because after the two years I will be able to go into several different fields that are interesting.

Doyle Hastings

For Exploration and Discussion

1. Consult the *Occupational Outlook Handbook* (Washington, D.C.: U.S. Government Printing Office, latest edition) to become better acquainted with this source of vocational information, giving particular attention to the information on specific careers of interest to you. Notice the DOT code number under each occupational title.

2. Study the *Dictionary of Occupational Titles* (DOT) (3rd edition. Washington, D.C.: U.S. Government Printing Office, 1965)

to determine how to use it effectively. In Volume I, each occupation is defined in a short paragraph and the work assigned a code number; sometimes the occupations are referred to as "three-digit classifications" and "six-digit classifications"; each digit has a specific meaning, the first digit referring to the major category; the next two digits, subgroups; and the last three digits indicating specific occupations within the subgroups, so that the three-digit classifications refer to groups of occupations and the six-digit classifications refer to individual occupations.

Start with Volume II and examine the list of three-digit occupational groups (pp. 3-24), copying down the occupational groups which interest you. With the selected three-digit code number, turn to a more detailed list of occupations (pp. 32-213) which come under the group you have selected, listing the ones that you wish to consider, and obtaining the six-digit codes. With these, refer back to volume I for definitions.

Continue your research in Volume II by examining the worker-trait groups on pp. 213-529. For experience, read the worker-trait information on the occupations of interior design and of motion picture camera work. For determining exact information on these two careers, look up the meaning of the code under "Qualification Profile" found on pp. 649-656. Then, research also the worker traits for the occupations that most interest you.

3. Investigate a career library at your college or in the community to find the occupational information available on films, tapes, or in pamphlets, books, and periodicals. In the main library, peruse the reference room, the catalogue, and the stacks for career information.

4. Write term papers on the two vocations you consider to be your first and second choices. Use many sources of information, including at least three interviews. Also list your bibliography.

In each paper refer to your aptitudes, interests, and temperament as they relate to your career choice; in your conclusion give your judgment of the suitability of the career for you.

Present your findings orally to the class.

5. To develop confidence and skill, try interviews in role-play situations.

Interview the instructor to explore the career of college teaching.

Invite a graduate of the school, now working in a successful career, to the class to be interviewed by all members.

References

1. J. Leonard Steinberg, *Guide to Careers through College Majors* (San Diego: Robert R. Knapp, Publisher, 1964).

2. Vernon H. Reeves, *Your College Degree* (Chicago: Science Research Associates, Inc., 1968).

3. Max F. Baer and Edward C. Roeber, *Occupational Information* (Chicago: Science Research Associates, Inc., 1964), pp. 313-314.

4. Peter M. Sandman, *Unabashed Career Guide* (New York: Macmillan Company, 1969).

PART III
Making the Choice

12

Meeting the Requirements

Choosing a career that is appropriate, appealing, and possible means accepting the responsibility for succeeding in that career by acquiring the necessary training and education. Choice signifies commitment to a career.

Preparation for a career is actually a part of the choosing process, because the worker's specific tasks in any field are determined by his level of competence and preparedness. The competence with which you enter your career is dependent not only upon your choice of work, but your choice of the training institution and the specialty you pursue within it. During your training period your work choice may be further modified as you gain more insight into your own abilities, or as circumstances influence your decisions.

Education and Training Programs

To increase your education and training there are several possibilities you may consider.

1. *Apprenticeship programs* are offered as cooperative ventures between education and industry. The young person who is accepted learns a trade by working on

the job, supervised and trained by his employer. At the same time, he attends school in the local junior college or other institution, often on week nights, taking courses in related subjects. The average apprenticeship is four years; the worker is paid a wage while he learns and, upon graduation, becomes a journeyman with a substantial income. The primary objective of the apprenticeship program is to train efficiently, to the degree of competence ordinarily expected of journeymen, the proper number of youths to meet the need for workers in such skilled occupations as cabinet making and millwork, carpentry, electric wiring, machine shop, surveying, meat cutting, plumbing, and sheet metal. (1) The young person who has enjoyed industrial arts experiences should consider this program. He would be screened through tests and during a probationary period of 30 to 90 days, according to the occupation, to give him a concept of what is expected of him in the occupation and to evaluate his suitability. Joint Apprenticeship Committees found in most cities take applications and make arrangements for screening. In New York State, the Bureau of Apprenticeship Training has established standards for over 300 skilled trades in apprenticeable careers which are listed with the years of training required in Lovejoy's *Career and Vocational School Guide.* (2)

2. There are career opportunities with the *military service* in many divergent areas. Information concerning the programs available may be found at local recruiting offices of the various services. Urgently needed are women nurses, dieticians, occupational and physical therapists. To students who will agree to serve in the Armed Forces, financial assistance is available in certain of the medical programs.

3. Many *private enterprises* offer industrial training to individuals with specific aptitudes and interests. Major utility and manufacturing companies frequently operate in-service training programs for employees or encourage their employees to attend college classes granting them work time or payment of fees.

4. Upon payment of tuition, *private training schools* prepare students for an occupation in the shortest possible time in such areas as business, barbering, modeling, and interior decorating.

5. *Technical institutes* give intensive courses concentrating almost entirely on technical skills. In some areas, Vocational-Technical schools are geared to the work available in the community where the school is located. For more detailed information, the State Employment Service maintains a directory of technical schools.

6. Finally, there are the publicly supported, low fee, *higher education institutions* available to nearly everyone. Universities, state colleges, and junior colleges cooperate in offering a great variety of educational programs at all levels. Universities offer the Bachelor's, Master's, and Doctor's degrees, and place emphasis on the graduate school program. State colleges offer the Bachelor's and Master's degrees, often specializing in the preparation of teachers. *Two-year colleges*, rapidly increasing across the nation, offer programs for transfer, general, vocational or technical education and they grant the Associate in Arts degree.

Until recently, choice of career was often determined an individual's inability to go to school or otherwise acqui the proper training. In some cases the necessary motivati was lacking. During the past decade greater opportunities f educational advantages have been extended to all people as part of national policy. Two key committees, the Nationa Planning Association and the National Committee on Tech nology, Automation, and Economic Progress, urged the estab lishment of universal higher education for all high schoo graduates. Making educational opportunity a citizen's right rather than a privilege, developed because of the emphasis upo our society's needs to fully develop all its human resources After World War II and the Korean War the GI Bill demor strated that a great variety of people can and will profit fro increased educational participation.

Financial Assistance

To increase educational opportunities, in 1958 Congress made available to college students large sums of money through a student loan program.

Loans under the National Defense Education Act (NDEA) vary in amounts up to $500 a semester to a needy, able student and can be continuous throughout his college years. Repayment of the loan begins one year after the borrower ceases to be a half- or full-time student and must be paid within ten years. No interest on the student loan may accrue before the beginning of the repayment period and interest thereafter is to be repaid at the rate of 3 per cent a year. The borrower's obligation to repay his loan is cancelled in the event of his death or permanent disability. The NDEA contains a further provision that up to 50 per cent of a loan may be cancelled if the borrower becomes a full-time teacher in a public elementary or secondary school. Recognizing the worth of such assistance, over 100,000 students borrowed $50,000,000 to finance their education during the first year of the program.

Through subsequent legislation the Congress has made available to students large grants of money which are matched by the college in work-study programs. Instead of borrowing the money, the student earns it by working for the college, either on or off campus. Other sums available through local banks are low-interest-rate loans underwritten by the national government.

Scholarships are offered by state governments, industry, community groups, and colleges. The admission officer of a private university said that because of increased grants-in-aid not one of his 10,000 member student body would need to withdraw because of financial need.

Another source of financial assistance is available for veterans under Public Law 89-358. For each month of active service up to 18 months, the serviceman is accorded one and one-half months of educational benefits; for service of 18 months or over he is entitled to benefits for 36 months. The law grants a monthly allowance to help meet the cost of subsistence, tuition, fees, books, and supplies; the amount allotted is on a sliding scale varying with the number of dependents and the number of course units. Education or training with veterans benefits is offered in colleges, apprenticeship programs, farm cooperatives, and flight training schools. More explicit information may be obtained directly from a Veterans Administration Office.

Because loans, scholarships, and awards rarely, if ever, are sufficient to pay all college expenses, your choice of college or training school may be influenced by total costs. If you have a job or are living at home, going away to school may not be feasible; in that event, you should investigate educational institutions nearest your home.

If you need financial assistance you should check with the college you wish to enter for further information on scholarships and awards, or write to the NEA Research Division in Washington, D.C., for a *Guide to Sources of Information on Scholarships*, or read Lovejoy's *Scholarship Guide*. In addition, you should consult a college counselor or financial aids officer.

The Community College

The public two-year college is a growing institution that provides a satisfactory education for a great variety of students. Termed a *community college* by the President's Commission on Higher Education in 1947, this preferred term is used here to identify what has commonly been called a junior college or a city college. Usually, the community college offers a diverse and comprehensive educational program, including special sequences in occupational, technical, general, and transfer education. These may lead to either an Associate in Arts (AA) degree or a Certificate of Achievement. This diversity characterizes its uniqueness, and enables the community college to function well in meeting the complex needs of all the community.

Edmund Gleazer, Jr., Executive Director of the American Association of Junior Colleges, describes the dramatic growth of the community college:

> Ten years ago one out of five students in the nation began his work in a community college. Now the number is more than one out of three. Soon it will be one out of two. During a time called "the age of education" this is one of the big stories. Here is a new kind of college. . . . Higher education was one parent; secondary education, the other. But the product of the union claims recognition in its own right, has an identity of its own — as robust offspring are wont to do." (3)

In California, there are over ninety junior colleges enrolling more than half a million students; 75 per cent of all full time lower division students attend a community college. In New York, 85 per cent of the residents are within commuting distance of a public, two-year college; in Florida, it is 99 per cent. These states, with the addition of Michigan, Illinois, Texas and Pennsylvania, seven states in all, contain 40 per cent of the population of this country. In each of these states policy has been adopted which will make community colleges available to all residents. (4)

With growing awareness of the value of the community colleges to their constituents, the Congress passed legislation for the first time in 1963 referring specifically to public community colleges and earmarking grant money for them. Successive laws expanded their support. (5) The members of the community, however, were the catalysts who voted for the community college and attended it.

> Although the recommendations of prestigious national committees and the activities of an educationally minded Congress gave a big boost to its growth, the real push came from the people. . . . The community college had its force and meaning rooted in the urgent needs of community life, in the process of change, and in the faith that among the ways to a better life none was more important than education. (6)

An open-door admissions policy permits anyone to register who can benefit from instruction, generally a high school graduate or a nongraduate over 18. The broad array of courses serves people of all ages, aptitudes, and goals: the Late Bloomer, the Drop Out, the Fall Out, the housewife, the disadvantaged, the returned veteran, the high school student with honor grades. Emphasis is not on past performance but on interest and effort. Although certain programs and courses within the college are selective, anyone may try to meet the requirements. If he fails, alternate programs may suit his potential and his purpose.

Grading policy matches the intent of the community college—to encourage students to try. Positive, flexible grading is the rule. Students have options: to withdraw after several weeks, to request credit/no-credit grading, or to aim for honor grades. Negative grading is disappearing. As faculty and trustees realize that failure to satisfactorily complete a course is penalty enough, the grade of "W" (withdrawal), or "N" (no grade) is replacing the penalizing "F".

Many community college programs prepare the student for immediate employment upon graduation, generally in the semiprofessional or technical and occupational fields where business, industry, and the professions look to the college for trained, capable personnel. Each community college does not offer training in every kind of occupation, but adjoining colleges supplement each other to offer all the needed programs.

Opportunities at a Community College

If you visited a community college campus and explored the facilities in order to sense the breadth of the offerings, this is what you might see:

In the public health services, scores of young women and some young men in their nursing uniforms are preparing to leave for a nearby hospital, participating in field work for the RN degree. In the dental assistant's office, a bustling preparation is being made for x-ray appointments, with some girls officiating at the counter and others at the machine.

A demonstration is in process in the electronics department of the latest transistor devices. Next door in vacuum technology you may hear an explanation of the moon shot into the vacuum of outer space.

The business department may be running a model office with "trained personnel" responsible for all activities of an operating firm. Marketing majors are working, being paid as they are trained in effective salesmanship. Data processing majors are feeding a computer occupying half of a large-size room; a continuous clicking breaks the silence of their concentration.

In welding design, flashing lights cast eerie shadows as arc welders fuse copper on zinc. Among the welding majors are a few art majors wishing to perfect their skills in metal sculpture.

Crossing campus, you might see law enforcement students in uniform checking student parking, here and there leaving a note of warning. In sharp contrast, on the lawn, nursery school assistants engage in creative play with happy children.

You cannot see all of it in one morning. The typical community college offers from 30 to 60 vocational and technical programs.

One community college in Modesto, California, a rural town, offers an AA degree program in agriculture with majors in such specialties as animal husbandry, horticulture, forestry, agricultural technology, and the dairy industry. Students from other junior colleges may enroll here through inter-district agreements or local district financing.

For continuing expansion, citizens' committees, alert to the needs of the community, suggest new majors; these are studied, developed, and eventually added to the curriculum. In New York, a community college serves the fashion industry, through its school the Fashion Institute of Technology.

Organized two-year curricula at Pasadena City College (1968) leading to an AA degree with vocational preparation included these majors:

Accounting
Architectural Specifications
Art—Advertising Design
Art—Apparel Arts

Art—Crafts
Art—Drawing and Painting,
   Printmaking, Sculpture
Art—Fashion Coordinating

continued

Art—Interior Design
Art—Photography
Automobile Mechanics
Building Construction
Business and Industrial
    Security
Business Data Processing
Business Management
Chemical Instrumentation
    Technology
Civil Engineering
    Technology
Clerical
Construction Inspection
Data Analysis and
    Processing
Dental Assisting
Dental Laboratory
    Technology
Drafting
Drafting—Aerospace Design
Drama
Electronic Engineering
    Technology
Electronics
Electronics—TV Technology
Fire Science
Forestry—Technical
Home and Family
Industrial Supervision
Instrument Engineering
    Technology

Insurance
Insurance Adjusting
Journalism
Library Technician
Machine Shop Practice
Marketing—Work Study
Medical Assisting
Merchandising
Metal Processes Technology
Nuclear Technology
Nursery School Assistant
Nursing, Registered
Nursing, Vocational
Photography
Police Science
Printing
Purchasing and Contracting
Real Estate
Recreation Leadership
Restaurant Operation
Secretarial
Secretarial Administration
Secretarial—Legal
Secretarial—Medical
Sign Art
Stewardess—Airline
Telecommunications—
    Control
Telecommunications—
    Production
Urban Community
    Development

Majors in aeronautics, food services, hotel management, inhalation therapy, or welding would attend another community college.

Students feel free to "sample" courses, to explore fields of knowledge, to examine several options in community colleges. During the same semester, a student may enroll in "Introduction to Data Processing," "Principles of Sales," and "Introduction to Law Enforcement." To help decide between vocational and RN degree nursing, another student could attempt "Anatomy and Physiology" or "Bacteriology." Many students challenge their academic interests and proficiencies before deciding between the two-year and four-year programs.

In addition to the occupational AA degree program, the community college offers special certificate programs and retraining programs for those who have been displaced from their present jobs or delayed in their advancement. These limited programs, recommended by the industries concerned, are usually a selected part of the regular AA curriculum.

General Education

General education is another type of community college offering. Some employers, such as the airlines, require their workers to be flexible, knowledgeable, and resourceful, specifying only an AA degree. General education, including communication, fine arts, and social studies, is of necessity a part of every AA major; the general nature of the knowledge helps the worker to accommodate to changes in his own career specialty as well as extend his cultural horizons.

In addition, the lower division program in specializations such as preengineering, business, or law, contains many of the same required general education courses. A student may change majors with little or no penalty at this level. Two semesters of science, a year of English and speech, three semesters of social science and some humanities are the usual requirements for the BA. This liberal pattern of general education broadens the perspective of the young student; the potential scholar may discover that he has fallen in love with a discipline he will pursue all his life; the prospective teacher may find his field of concentration; the business student may discover his greatest interest; and the naturalist may find new enthusiasm as preparing for a career becomes a part of the choosing. Some decisions will be made, tentative and open to review, during the general education program in your first two years of college.

Unpredicted enrollments in the fine arts encouraged some departments to develop extensive facilities which enrich the general education offerings. Music departments, for example, organize symphony orchestras, opera workshops, and jazz festivals. Recognizing and relishing the opportunity to be creative, today's youth enroll in many art classes at the community college. In one extended day class in ceramics, students pooled their clay and molded a life-size Volkswagen (using a car as a mold), inflicting it with the marks of carnage on the highway. Community life as well as individual life is enriched by these programs.

If two years of college is all you can spend on your preparation for a career, at least for now, the AA degree may fulfill your purpose. If your goal requires a BA degree then your community college preparation must be a transfer program.

The Transfer Program

The community college offers a complete lower division curriculum for a Bachelor of Arts (BA) degree, permitting the qualified student to transfer to a four-year college or university. Because one-third of all students enrolled in the community college complete this transfer program and enter a four-year institution, community college offerings in various departments parallel basic university courses. In this way, for example, engineering students receive the proper chemistry, and business students study some humanities.

Because of flexible general education programming, there recently has been a move toward liberalization of the transfer process. Some four-year colleges now request that community college transcripts be evaluated by the community college and stamped "General Education Completed" in order to be accepted without comparison or deletion of units. The trend is to transfer all credits, with the exception of remedial courses, but including credits from technical and vocational courses.

Transfers may suffer little or no loss of credits or course work. Many states have established a Master Plan of Higher Education, assigning to each institution a specific purpose. In

Cleveland, Ohio, the State University and the community college developed a detailed plan of partnership. The community college is the center for freshman and sophomore courses, offering, in addition, occupational education; the university concentrates on upper division programs and graduate and professional schools, enrolling freshmen and sophomores on a limited basis. The two institutions have developed joint counseling services, assisting each student to select the program and school that he needs.

....

Cooperation Between Colleges   One ambitious young man arranged to study for his Master's degree in engineering at the state college and then to cross town to the community college to continue a program in electronics. He explained that the theory at the university without the practical application at the community college left him insecure in his field.

....

Eighty per cent of the students who transfer to a four-year institution are awarded the BA degree. In a study of the transfer student, Knoell and Medsker reported that all or most junior college students could be successful in achieving their degree goals after transfer if they would select four-year institutions and major fields which are appropriate to their ability and prior achievement. (7) In the California state colleges, a report from the Chancellor titled "Those Who Made It" shows that of all those who received their BA degree, 44 per cent started in community colleges.

Sometimes the transfer student remains at the community college for three or four years, making up deficiencies in his high school preparation. Or he must work; over one-half of community college students hold part time jobs. Some students work full time supporting a family, and continuing their studies with six or nine units a semester. Husband and wife teams are not uncommon, sharing books, classes, and trading off babysitting responsibilities. The opportunity to obtain a BA degree in a liberal arts college may be possible only because the flexible programming at the community college enables the serious student to complete his first two years at a low cost and at his own pace.

Fortune may determine that you spend your first two years at a four-year school. Here too you can hold open your options while you explore your abilities and continued interest in your chosen field. Sink or swim, you may delve into your program with vigor.

....

Change of Major   His first year of college, Sam attended university on a scholarship. Filled with confidence, he registered for an overload of engineering courses. At the end of the first semester he had two D's on his record, and was told that he must make two B's the following term to maintain his scholarship. He received all C's. When he enrolled at City College the next year, he commented ruefully, "I'm going back to the university; they'll save the scholarship for me, but I've switched my major to chemistry."

....

Choice of Major

A choice of major is a part of occupational choice and is often made while completing the general education requirements. A major in political science may be a "dead end" unless you plan to be a college professor or lawyer. The major in humanities may have difficulty finding a career job; he might teach, but probably even this would require graduate work in a concentrated field. The social science major can select social service, teaching, government work, and research. The home economics major may choose food and clothing, industrial planning, clinical dietetics, teaching at all levels, and child care. The mathematics major may choose between pure and applied mathematics as he selects research, teaching, consultation, or management of scientific affairs. Being on the right road is a critical part of reaching the hoped-for destination with ample choice and thorough preparation.

Obtaining a degree in a specific major, however, does not mean that you are limited unconditionally to that area for your career choice. An awakened, knowledgeable, trained mind is an asset in any work and there are some persons who need the entire four-year college experience to absorb knowledge on which to move into their chosen realm of work. The primitive art major may go into business; the business major often turns to economics; the lawyer may have his major in almost any subject. When a music major graduate discovered that his comprehension of note reading was invaluable in data programming he found exciting, rewarding work as a programmer for an international business concern. If you are still searching for a vocational area, you will have options open after you are graduated that can lead to satisfying work choice.

Your choice of major may influence your choice of college, because many colleges have a specialty. Some majors, such as oceanography, forestry, architecture, dental hygiene, and data processing are offered in only selected institutions. California publishes a guidebook to the four-year colleges within that state, *Counselors Guide to College Majors*, listing by degree major all the schools that offer that major. Barron's *Guide to the Two-Year Colleges* and Lovejoy's *College Guide* give comparable information for colleges in all of the states. Find out as much as you can about the college with your specialty. Consult the college catalog, visit the school, if possible, and talk to graduates. Instructors and counselors, particularly any who have attended the school, may have some useful advice.

Some schools with highly specialized majors have a limited enrollment and a stringent admission policy. A pediatrician, addressing a college class on careers in medicine, said that he was 27 when he returned from selective service and applied to medical school. Universities in his home state on the West Coast refused him admission because he was too old. "As a result," he said, "I got in my wheel chair and went to a medical school in a mid-eastern state."

Which College?

The four-year college has the prestige that many students court. Two-thirds of the students, as a rule, enter the community college hoping and planning to transfer to the four-year institution. In actuality, one-third will do so, a comparable attrition to that of freshmen in the four-year schools.

Acceptance as a part of the master plan of higher education has raised the status of the community college. Realizing the value of this institution to the community and to all of education, universities and state colleges have opened the channels of communication, advising and assisting administrators, faculty, and students.

More money from the state and more concern from the community has resulted in expanded curricula. Typical new course offerings include: "American Indian Ethnology," a study of Indian culture prior to settlement by the white man; "Community Organization," a study of urban sprawl, emphasizing the growth of the ghetto; "Black Culture," "Afro-American History," "Introduction to African History," "Mexican Sociology," and "Spanish for Bilinguals."

As never before, Americans believe that the individual should develop his potential to the fullest; any other goal is wasteful, careless, and improperly motivated.

Gleazer succinctly sums up the situation:

> Occupational education needs to be examined closely enough to see it is a broad and complex field that requires not only manual, manipulative, and communication skills, but also academic abilities similar to those of the transfer liberal arts student. . . . To assign the weak student to an occupational education is no answer. He may find a program within occupational education which is right for him but the field in general requires as wide a spectrum of aptitudes and abilities as is needed in the transfer program — maybe wider. . . .
> [Wherever one goes, to the junior college, state college, or university, the goals will in significant ways be the same]: to learn to support oneself, to contribute toward society's corporate life, and to develop social perspective and compassion. (8)

For Exploration and Discussion

1. Do some research in a school directory such as Lovejoy's *Career Guide* or Barron's *Guide to the Two Year Colleges.* Specifically read to discover the kind of information that this gives; check accuracy by reading about the colleges nearest you.

2. Watch for articles in the newspaper and in periodicals on the community colleges, the state colleges, and the universities. Observe any trends in policy, curriculum, and fees.

3. Read *This is the Community College* by Edmund Gleazer (Boston: Houghton-Mifflin Company, 1968).

4. In the main library or career library, spend an hour looking through recent college catalogues.

5. Consult with a counselor on the colleges that are outstanding in your major; consult him also to find out the kind of financial assistance available.

6. In your educational planning, devise a four-semester program that would lead to a two-year college degree with occupational training and that could serve also as the first two years of a four-year Bachelor of Arts degree, for example, an AA degree in Engineering Drafting and an Industrial Arts BA degree. With how many two-year college programs could this be accomplished?

7. Compare the advantages of a four-year apprenticeship training program to the advantages of a two-year community college occupational training program and degree.

8. If the community college nearest you does not offer the particular major of most interest to you, visit those near to you which do offer it.

9. Visit the state university. If you know someone who attends there have him show you around the campus or perhaps visit on a Career or Visitation Day. Collect and read the free literature, school paper, and bulletins to catch the campus atmosphere.

10. If meeting the requirements seems to you to be too difficult or to require too many years of your life, ask yourself these questions and discuss them with your friends:
    a. Will the time you are in school or training be any longer or shorter because you are so occupied?

    b. At the end of six years, perhaps, will you look back over those years and regret them?

    c. Can meeting the requirements be a "now" experience, through awareness and imaginative planning?

References

1. California State Department of Education, *Apprenticeship Handbook for Education* (Sacramento, Calif.,: The Department, 1964), p. 3.

2. Clarence E. Lovejoy, *Lovejoy's Career and Vocational School Guide* (New York: Simon and Schuster, 1967).

3. Edmund Gleazer, *This is the Community College* (Boston: Houghton Mifflin Company, 1968), p. 4.

4. Gleazer, pp. 26-27.

5. Gleazer, p. 15.

6. Gleazer, pp. 16, 20.

7. Dorothy M. Knoell and Leland L. Medsker, *From Junior to Senior College: A National Study of the Transfer Student* (Washington D.C.: American Council on Education, 1965).

8. Gleazer, pp. 73, 79.

13

Industry, Business, Government, the Professions or Paraprofessions?

In addition to choosing the activity that you prefer for your working life, you also must choose the setting for work and the organization of work. All work takes place within an environment and all work is organized. Both environment and organization contain significant details dictating the kinds of workers that are required.

The *organization* is defined as the type of management. Industries and businesses, large and small, are controlled by corporations, companies, partnerships, or single owners; federal, state, or local government by elected and appointed officials; the professions by the self-employed, with partners, or as a part of a larger organization. In each type of organization will be found paraprofessionals or technicians.

During your lifetime you may experience several kinds of organized work. For assistance, you can receive warning or encouragement from the work experiences of others, but you must evaluate different kinds of organized work in terms of the changing times and with recognition of your personal preferences and needs.

The most likely place for you to find employment, considering sheer numbers, is in industry or government. As you near the completion of your education and training, companies will solicit your application. Unless you have thought through your choice of working situations and work organization, you may feel as though you are gambling; before you is a wheel of choice and not a wheel of chance. It will be to your advantage to study all the options.

Recruitment

Because industries need fresh, innovative young workers, they will compete for your services. Increasing pressure to find trained personnel has led industry to develop new and better ways to reach and influence available trainees, as a beginning, with audio-visual devices, seminars, and exhibits at Career Forums. Then, the big companies send recruiters to the college campuses; facile young men study transcripts, conduct interviews, make decisions, reinterview and then make offers.

Though the two-year college does not receive as solicitous attention from the industrial world as four-year colleges, companies do contact departments of vocational education each spring to recruit applicants for their employment needs. Often applicants are seduced from their education and training before they receive the AA degree, but those who remain to complete the four-semester program are carefully placed by their instructors in select companies. One electronics department takes its graduates on a tour of the plants of potential employers, visiting the research and development areas, where nearly all of the graduates are placed.

For some reason, careful screening is not always successful; recurring studies show that 50 per cent of the selected college graduates leave their jobs by the third year, 67 per cent by the fourth year, and 73 per cent by the fifth year. (1) Interviews to identify the reasons for their leaving uncovered a lack of understanding by the students of both the company and their position in it. Dissatisfaction was not with the salary nor promotions but with their own lack of personal development. What they wanted, they said, was:

1. A chance to test themselves by making a meaningful contribution to the company efforts.

2. An opportunity to learn and grow and make use of their personal abilities and education.

3. The right to retain their integrity and individuality and not be forced to conform to a company pattern or be brainwashed into an organization man mentality.

4. The opportunity to be a part of a dynamic company, receptive to new ideas. (2)

To remedy this tenuous placement, some companies are sending line executives in place of recruiters to hire students for their own departments.

Before employment, however, you need to take the responsibility for investigating the companies you are considering for employment. Your questions might be: "What is the management's philosophy?" "Is the company person-oriented?" "Has the company hired graduates from my school and has their record been good?" "Do the company requirements really match my job objectives?"

Investigating Possible Employment

You will find help in investigating companies through the College Placement Council, Inc. Each year the Council publishes and distributes free of charge the *College Placement Annual*, a large volume containing the employment needs of 2,100 companies and government agencies. This volume gives an introduction to a majority of companies in the country and describes briefly each organization and its openings. Generally, a BA degree is necessary to apply for these positions, but with the surge in technical and paraprofessional workers, many companies should be considered as possible employers by community college graduates.

Craftsmen — plumbers, draftsmen, welders, printers, barbers, auto mechanics, machinists, and carpenters—are selected by companies who depend on personal recommendations as well as grades, interviews, and test scores as criteria for employment. To be a part of a reputable company, well established in the community, is significant for the ambitious craftsman. Consequently, he, too, must investigate organizations to discover which ones can offer him the opportunities he seeks — to be a part of and share in a competent, respected company.

Another volume, the *Macmillan Job Guide to American Corporations* (Ernest McKay, ed., New York: Macmillan Company, 1967), contains a "complete profile of 260 top US corporations with capsule commentaries on job opportunities in 50 states and overseas." Actually, the exact purpose of this book is to give the college student a more accurate picture of a company and its function before he applies for a job. With this in mind, the editor includes brief histories, descriptions, and statements of purpose as well as detailed explanations of degree requirements and opportunities. In the book, companies may be identified through three indexes: alphabetical, geographical, and vocational. The vocational index crosses all industry lines. More than 120 disciplines are specifically mentioned as a necessary or preferred academic background for employment. If you wish to know more, you will find for each company the number of employees, the revenue sales, and the location of subsidiary plants. Most libraries have this book for reference.

The value of researching companies lies in knowing what the choices are and in relating this knowledge to your own aims and purposes.

Big Companies versus Small Companies

How small is small? In the Small Business Administration's lending program, a manufacturing firm is considered small if it has 100 or fewer employees and large if it has more than 1000 employees, the size standard being related to the

Table 9
Sample Organization Chart of a Large Manufacturing Company

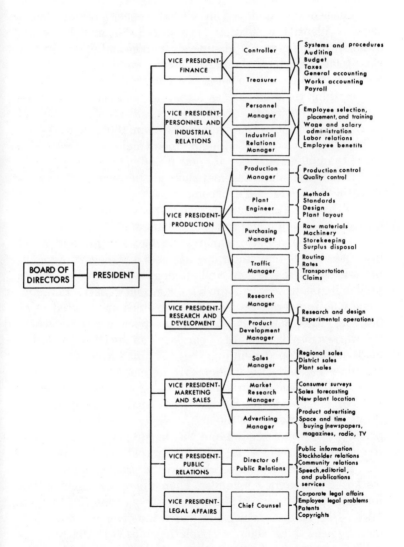

kind of industry. In a small company the owners are usually the managers, the capital is held by a small group, and the area of operation is local, but the market may be widespread.

The worker employed in a small concern usually has a sense of identity with what is produced. He may know the owners, the managers, and supervisors personally, and in this close relationship, his ability and growth will be assessed. It is generally true that the owners who personally know their men will care for their employees during a slack season. Surprisingly, small businesses account for a substantial portion of total employment: firms with fewer than 100 employees account for 41 per cent of all paid employment, and those with fewer than 500 employees account for 56 per cent. (3) ·

Often, the small business succeeds because of the excellence of its product. To become a part of such a company means that the craftsman or businessman enjoys this reputation and shares in maintaining and extending it.

There is a definite demarcation between big and small business. As you may know, big business is strongest in manufacturing, transportation, and mining; while small business predominates in service industries, contract construction, and wholesale and retail trades. Big companies are located in or near big cities. Some have subsidiaries in smaller towns where the worker may be proud to "check in" at the office located in modern, landscaped buildings, eat his lunch in a colorful immaculate cafeteria, and take part in recreation club activities. He may speak with pride of being employed at GE or IBM or Lockheed. But he never sees what his company produces; he may never see the entire plant; he doesn't know the president. His pay is good and the benefits are numerous but the loss of a government contract may cost him his job.

With the right connections and the proper motivation, a worker may become a manager. There are many opportunities for such positions in big companies if one has the "savoir-faire." See Table 9, which illustrates the diverse functions of management and their interrelationships. (4) Big business needs aspiring young executives. With this aspiration the worker again must assess his values; his time, dedication and attitudes must serve the new master; he must be sure such loyalty is worthy.

Self-Employment

In the world of work, an individual may elect to go into business for himself—to be an entrepreneur who undertakes the risk and responsibility of managing his own concern. Admittedly, this is not for the majority of workers. For those who select it, however, entrepreneurship, or self-employment, is a satisfactory and interesting, even exciting, way of life.

First of all, the independent man of business is a leader. He directs and controls what is accomplished. Since this accomplishment is usually for the good of the community as well as his employees, he is also a leader in the community who is respected and consulted on community affairs. For those who seek business ownership, this may be the most gratifying of all rewards.

Independence is characteristic of the successful businessman. He enjoys and seeks the responsibility of dealing with suppliers, directing employees, satisfying customers, and managing his affairs. He relies on his own judgment, takes the initiative, presses for results, and secures the reward. The excitement and intrigue are like that in the sports arena. If he wins, he gains financial and social benefits and a sense of service.

He may lose. He may lose his personal savings. He may have to work long hours to safeguard his investment. During the slack season he must curtail his expenditures and watch his cash, but the successful entrepreneur has calculated upon these eventualities. Because the knowledge and experience of being his own man dwarfs other considerations, he accepts the ebb and flow of his existence with equanimity.

Seldom does a young person plunge into business for himself without previous experience in the service of another. It is this training that enables him to judge the hazards and obstacles and demands of ownership. Unless he plans to take part in a family enterprise or an inherited proprietorship, he must also work to save the necessary capital.

Government Service

The biggest employer in the United States is the government. When all workers at the federal, state, and local level are included, the government employs one out of every seven workers.

The federal government competes for workers just as industry does; in the *College Placement Annual,* published annually by the College Placement Council, Inc., Bethlehem, Pennsylvania, are listings describing the employment opportunities in the various departments and agencies of the federal government with the name and address of the personnel officer to contact.

Lincoln once said, "The legitimate object of government is to do for the people what needs to be done, but which they cannot, by individual effort, do at all, or do so well themselves."

The departments and agencies of the federal government reflect this concern for human welfare; in naming them, the scope of national concern is evident:

1   Department of Health, Education and Welfare
1a Food and Drug Administration
1b Social Security Administration
2   Department of Housing and Urban Development
3   Department of the Interior
3a Bureau of Indian Affairs
3b Bureau of Mines
3c Geological Survey
3d Bureau of Reclamation
4   Department of Justice
4a Immigration
4b Naturalization Service
4c Federal Bureau of Prisons
5   Department of Labor
6   Department of State
7   Department of Transportation
7a Federal Aviation Administration
8   Department of the Treasury
8a Internal Revenue Service
9   Post Office Service
10 Department of Defense
10a Central Intelligence Agency

11 Department of Agriculture	12 Department of Commerce
11a Forestry Service	12a National Bureau of Standards
11b Consumer and Marketing Service (which administers the school lunch and food stamp programs)	12b Patent Office
	12c Economic Development Administration

In addition to these areas, special agencies have made headlines the last few years: the National Aeronautics and Space Administration (NASA); Veterans Administration; the Office of Economic Opportunity and its War on Poverty; the Peace Corps, and VISTA, now combined in ACTION.

Every kind of trained personnel is needed to man this comprehensive, complex ship of state. The chairman of the United States Civil Service Association, John W. Macy, Jr., wrote:

> Government is plumbing the oceans and exploring outer space, conducting cancer research and studying new techniques in scientific farming, improving flight safety by technology and regulations, and ushering in the era of space communication. All these ventures and many more require not only talented scientists but also skilled managers. (5).

The Department of Agriculture in its request for recruits reports,

> The United States Department of Agriculture serves all Americans and meets human needs across the globe. Utilizing nearly all skills, it is staffed by men and women in 50 states and 65 foreign countries. Their mission is a better life — a better world. (6)

Some feel there is no basic difference between work in a private concern and work in the government; government employees simply choose to do their work in the public service. Public service calls for every kind of talent and training, such as: auditors, chemists, dentists, engineers, librarians, nurses, physicians, photographers, printers, psychologists, real estate appraisers, recreation therapists, soil experts, stenographers, surgeons, surveyors, teachers, typists, veterinarians. The government employs nearly every specialty from accounting to zoology. (7a) Federal employees are stationed in all parts of the United States, the territories, and many foreign countries.

Civil Service Examinations

To get a job with the federal government, it is necessary to take the civil service examination, a competitive examination to insure that employees will be selected on the basis of merit and fitness.

The Federal Service Entrance Examination is given nine times a year in 650 locations and, if you pass this two and one-half hour examination, your name is listed in the federal civil service register, qualifying you for two hundred federal jobs, at home and overseas. Eligible applicants are listed by their scores and the list is given to the appropriate agency who can select any one of the top three candidates. Names of those not selected are restored to the list for application to other job openings.

Other tests are given for specific job titles. Detailed information on civil service examinations, how to prepare for them, what they cover, and sample examinations may be found in several books printed in the *Arco Publishers Civil Service Test Series*, New York, and the *Ken Publishers Federal Examination Series*, San Francisco. The United States Civil Service Commission issues a pamphlet *Working for the USA* and other publications that are distributed at the application counter of any post office or regional center. Additional information may be obtained at the State Employment Service Center's and the Interagency Board System's complete one-step information centers located in large cities throughout the country.

State and Local Governments

Recently, a state senator was asked if he would run for a United States Senate seat which was soon to be vacant. "No," he replied, "I am closer to the people of my state when I live and work here."

One young woman spent a year as a fellow in the office of the Vice President of the United States. She assisted in many exciting activities including getting more money for the Mississippi Head Start Program. When she evaluated her internship, she spoke highly of some of the departments with broad involvement in social problems, but she concluded,

There is more action in the state and local governments because they offer a more direct approach to people and their problems, where you can reach out and find people who need help rather than just respond as does the federal government. (8)

State and local governments hold responsibility for such services as public health, social welfare, motor vehicles, water resources, public works, professional and vocational standards, parks and recreation, public employment, and education.

One state publication described the work in this manner,

Viewed in the light of "doing for the people what needs to be done" both the role of the state government and the service extended to the people gain greater and more specific significance.

The Highway Patrol becomes more than a law enforcement department — it is the officer rushing to the scene of an accident to give first aid to the injured. Fish and Game become more than another state office — it is the pilot flying an airplane to remote lakes to stock them with trout for a million anglers. The Department of Employment becomes more than state officers concerned with economic security — it is the interviewer in a state employment office advising applicants on Job opportunities in government and industry. (7b)

Benefits

With an expanding population and expanding services, government work, for the most part, is secure. Benefits are liberal, including pay equivalent to that of private industry, several weeks' vacation pay, a retirement system, and life and health insurance programs. Conversely, bureaucracy is the bane of government employment with its adherence to fixed rules and a hierarchy of authority where officialism, red tape, and proliferation can "hedge in" the creative worker.

If you plan to work in a department of government, choose one whose aim coincides with your own sense of purpose. If you can be creative within it, everyone will be served. Recently, young people have been stirring up action and ideas within the established system and dry, dusty offices are being rejuvenated. The stifling of creativity in young workers is actually a paradox because on one hand government and industry cry for "fresh young blood" with innovative ideas while on the other hand new recruits withdraw because they feel repressed. Fortunately, revolutionary change is in the air. With the new seriousness of youth toward civic and moral responsibility, it may be that their elders in positions of authority will permit them and even encourage them to breathe fresh life into crumbling cities and atrophying industries. There are instances of this happening. A twenty-five-year-old graduate took a leave of absence from his banking position to work on the campaign of the mayor of Indianapolis. In the excitement of the campaign, he became committed to urban problems. Consequently, he became the successful director of special projects encompassing the Model Cities program. (9) There are enough breakthroughs to enthusiastic enterprise to make any other way unacceptable.

The Professional

The professional is a specialist in one body of knowledge, such as law, medicine, teaching, dentistry, pharmacy, art, architecture, acting, and science. He must study beyond the BA degree, often in a select school. Generally he must face rigorous state examinations to obtain a license to practice. Although entrance into the professions was blocked in the past by the cost of attending the professional school and by restricted enrollment, the urgent need for professional people plus more financial and academic opportunities have helped to open the doors to more students.

Any young person who enjoys his academic work and earns honor grades should consider the professions. Long years of hard study are a part of the commitment, but if a person likes to study and readily masters the subject matter, the years go by and suddenly the goal is reached. The professional person is respected in society because he has mastered a body of knowledge which serves society. Doctors, lawyers, nurses, teachers, engineers are in the professional forefront for advancement of human welfare.

If you are considering one of the professions, you should become familiar with the professional life style. The life of the professional person, contrary to public opinion, is not an easy one. John Tebbel points out the paradox of the laboring man with shorter and shorter hours and the professional man with longer and longer hours. (10) With his sense of responsibility for serving clients in a burgeoning population, the professional has incredible demands upon his energy and time. He tries to protect himself by going into partnership and by supporting his professional organizations but these, too, are inadequate. In the end, he must resign himself to the fact that he is on constant call, that others must be served, and that his life is his career.

There are many joys in the life of the professional: the joy of helping others, the satisfaction of doing a difficult task, the pleasure of conferring with colleagues, and the continuing stimulation of advancing knowledge. There is variety in this life. No two days are the same and the pattern of each day is kaleidoscopic.

The bitter in the professional's life is the time he fails, for there will be such times. Misjudgment and other causes must be borne. A doctor of repute confessed with anguish that he wished he were a laborer the day he lost the first grandchild of his best friend. Likewise, teachers grieve for students who fail. And the mathematician sometimes recognizes many fruitless hours. The research scientist may bear the weight of the misuse of his efforts. But if he is equal to the demands thrust upon him, the professional has the "best of all possible worlds" in that he can fulfill himself in the nearly complete realization of his potential.

The Paraprofessional

Close to professionals are highly trained technicians. Engineers, doctors, and scientists are dependent for their functioning upon a coterie of specialists, highly trained in a broad range of complex skills. The Commission on Science Education described the *technician* in this manner:

> The highly trained technician has a broader range of complex skills than either the skilled craftsman or the engineer. His educational program is oriented toward scientific and technological theory but it is directed more toward application of theory than is the education of the engineer or scientist. Technical education programs can be classed very roughly into 1) those based on the physical sciences and engineering, 2) those based upon the biological sciences, and 3) those based upon both the physical and biological sciences. (11)

Technicians who work with engineers and scientists are representative of the relationship between the professional and his assistant. These para-professionals work both in research and development and in production. In the laboratory, they conduct experiments or tests; set up, calibrate, and operate instruments; and make calculations. They assist scientists and engineers by working under their direction to develop experimental equipment and models and to make drawings and sketches. Frequently they handle certain aspects of the design work, especially modifying designs for specific needs. In production they may follow a course laid out by the engineer, but often without close supervision. They may do the work of the engineer by advising on installation and maintenance problems, serving as technical sales and field representatives or working as technical writers of specification manuals.

Specialized training is part of the education given the technician in the area of technology in which he will work. He may work as a chemical technician, civil engineering technician, an industrial technician, an electronic technician, as a mechanical, metallurgical, mathematical, biological, agricultural, or instrumentation technician. For each one, a particular body of knowledge and highly developed set of skills are necessary.

The Commission on Science Education, through grants from the National Science Foundation, is conducting a study of the education of technicians. The first report emphasized that "technical education at the college level has emerged as a major component of American higher education," and "that a critical shortage of technicians will be as much a matter of national concern as was the shortage of scientists and engineers a few years ago." (12)

Because of the critical need for the development and improvement of technical education, Congress has made available large sums of money through the Vocational Education Amendments of 1968, administered by the US Office of Education (USOE). One of the recommendations is that special attention be given to the development of a "2 + 2" program so that graduates in a two-year college program can elect to continue to the baccalaureate degree in technology or can do so after a period of employment as technicians.

A new baccalaureate degree program in the departments of industry and technology is now being offered by many four-year colleges so that the person with two years of training in his area of interest (electronics, automotive, air conditioning and refrigeration, manufacturing, etc.) may transfer his course credits to the four-year college and continue his studies for the Bachelor of Science degree.

Technicians frequently are assuming some of the routine duties of the professional worker, freeing him for work requiring more education and training. The growing list of paraprofessionals includes: medical technologists, medical x-ray technicians, dental hygienists, medical record librarians, vacuum technologists, teaching assistants, vocational nurses, and engineer and science technicians.

In a recent report entitled "Twenty-five Technical Careers You Can Learn in Two Years or Less," the USOE stated that the demands for people with technical skills is growing twice as fast as for any other group, that there aren't enough applicants to fill technical positions, and that over 1,000,000 more will open by 1975. The report states that the way to break into any field—from medicine to computers to engineering to the space program—is to become a technician.

Types of Technicians

The types of technicians now in most demand and a brief description of the kinds of work they do are included here.

Aeronautical and Aerospace
Work on design of space vehicles, missiles, supersonic transports. Help solve air traffic control problems. Help explore space. The aeronautical and aerospace field is growing so quickly, these are just a few examples of the work this technician does.

Air Conditioning and Refrigeration
Help in the design of future astrodomes, spaceships, sea laboratories, ultramodern homes and cities under domes— the air-conditioning, refrigerating and heating systems of the future.

Agricultural
Work on the scientific production and processing of food and other things that grow. Act as consultant on farm machinery, agricultural chemicals and production techniques.

Architectural and Construction
Work on projects to rebuild cities. Develop new building techniques, and new materials for building. Through city planning, help with sociological problems that plague inner cities.

Automotive
Assist in the design of new traffic control systems. Help in the planning of tomorrow's cars, especially smog control devices, automatic guidance systems, and new safety features. Work on the problems of mass transport.

Chemical
Work in new fields of chemistry, especially biochemistry and chemical engineering. Help develop new materials

from chemicals, especially new plastics, new foods, new fertilizers, new anti-pollution agents.

Civil Engineering

Work in several branches, including 1) Structural Technology: work with computers to find new building techniques for skyscrapers, bridges, docks and related structures; 2) Highway Technology: work on roads, automated transportation, airports, and ports; 3) Surveying Technology: help map and develop unconquered territory in all parts of the world.

Commercial Pilot

Pilot airplanes and helicopters. Act as cabin crew in commercial aircraft. (These careers call for experience after a two-year educational program.)

Electrical

Work with new electrical devices such as portable power systems for use in remote areas, fuel cells for use in spaceships and sea labs. Help design electrical systems for tomorrow's homes and factories.

Electronic

Work with new electronic fields of miniaturization, solid-state devices. Work with scientists in new bioengineering systems. Work on fourth-generation computers, teaching machines, and other electronic machines.

Electromechanical

Help design new information systems, new computers. Work on artificial hearts, and other artificial human organs in the new field of biomedical technology. Work on automated production equipment.

Electronic Data Processing

Process and analyze business and scientific data using new generation computers. Develop new systems analysis to solve storage and retrieval problems. Help develop new teaching machines.

Fire Protection

Develop new fail-safe systems for supersonic transports, sea labs, and other artificial environments to make them safe for human habitation.

Forestry

Help care for, protect and harvest forests. Develop and conserve wildlife and recreational resources.

Health Service
Work with medical teams as assistant or nurse on the new frontiers of medicine. Work on bioengineering techniques to save and prolong life, as in inhalation therapy, radiation therapy, nuclear medicine techniques. Work in dentistry and oral surgery.

Industrial Production
Help design new production methods, automated systems, and new materials, machinery, and control systems to make industry more productive.

Instrumentation
Work on the instruments that have made possible space exploration, new medical techniques, automation, pollution control and other modern miracles.

Marine Life and Ocean Fishing
Develop new procedures for harvesting food from the ocean. Help discover new minerals beneath the sea. Work on conserving the ocean's natural resources.

Mechanical Design
Work on producing new kinds of machines for tomorrow's manufacturing plants, hospitals, and homes.

Metallurgical
Help develop and produce new "miracle" metals and metal alloys for use in construction, machinery, and medicine.

Nuclear and Radiological
Help research, develop and produce nuclear devices and atomic power plants. Use radio isotopes in industrial and health fields.

Oceanography
Explore the ocean's chemistry, geography and mineral resources. Develop ways to use them. Develop manned underwater sea labs.

Office Specialists
Accounting, financial control, and management. Scientific, legal, medical, or engineering secretaries.

Police Science
Work on new, scientific methods to detect and prevent crime.

Sanitation and Environmental Control
Help improve man's environment and protect natural resources by scientific means. Help prevent or control air

and water pollution. Inspect and prevent contamination of food. Control waste disposal. (13)

The Skilled Worker

In the field of industry, you may choose to be a craftsman in the production area rather than the business man, a professional or a technician. Persons with excellent hand and eye coordination or manual dexterity who enjoy seeing things made and making things work will find here many employment opportunities.

"The nation's economic strength depends to a great extent on the initiative and competence of the craftsman," explains the Department of Labor. "Skilled workers make the patterns, models, tools, dies, machines, and equipment without which industrial processes could not occur and, in addition, build the needed homes, commercial and industrial buildings and highways." (14)

Presently, there are over ten million skilled workers employed in almost every branch of industry, although two-thirds of the workers are employed in manufacturing and construction. More than four-fifths of the skilled workers are employed by private companies; others work for the government or are self-employed, often in the building trades. Skilled workers must have a thorough knowledge of the processes involved in their work, often must exercise independent judgment and may be responsible for valuable equipment or products. Consequently they require training to qualify for their jobs.

Training for skilled labor requires passing a test for the necessary aptitude. Many apprenticeship screening tests are given by the State Employment Services or local community colleges.

Vocational training centers, technical colleges, and community colleges offer extensive programs in skilled work fields, leading to the AA degree. Automotive technology, aviation mechanics, carpentry, drafting, tool design, welding design, graphic arts, and many other occupational curricula are available to persons with the appropriate abilities and interests.

Teaching Assistants and Teaching

In the field of education, the position of the paraprofessional, the teacher's aide and teaching assistant, was established in 1968 by the Education Profession Development Act. There are now 200,000 teacher aides in the United States; a recent prediction is that by 1977, there will be one and a half million, as a result of the encouraging reports from five states that indicate a distinct improvement of learning in children through the employment of instructional aides. New educational legislation provides for incorporating work-study opportunities into the program which would enable the new aides to progress to teaching assistants and professional teachers. (15)

The role of the teaching aide in some areas is to explain to the community what it must understand about the school and explain to the school what it must understand about the community by working with the parents as well as the children, even to the degree of teaching parents (accomplished with Puerto Rican families) to read to their children. From the standpoint of the schools, the use of para-professionals will provide a new and powerful link with the community, will compensate for present staff shortages, and could provide a marked decrease in pupil-teacher ratios. From the standpoint of the community, the para-professionals brought into the schools will gain skills and abilities and so build its human resources.

Should you consider the career of the teaching paraprofessional? The answer might be yes, if you are attracted to the profession because of the variety, service, and challenge offered in the work and because you cannot get the education and training needed for the career of the professional teacher. You may just prefer the active aspect of the profession in application of the theory rather than in developing it.

Of all the professions, teaching is the largest. Of all state employment, teaching has the greatest number. Positions in elementary, secondary, and college instruction are a polar variety, appealing to individual interests and tastes. The common denominator is an empathy bordering on compassion for those who are taught.

If there is one hope for improving the inequities of humanity, to many that hope is educational opportunity. There is a new working proposition in education that "any subject matter can be taught to anybody at any age in some form that is honest." (16) This startling premise is changing the conservative, constrained pedagogue into an experimenting, lively mentor. To recognize the fact that with sufficient effort and imagination any topic can be grasped by the mind of a child, an adolescent, or an adult if it is presented in an appropriate form opens up all sorts of innovations. Within his reach, the teacher has the technical wizardry of teaching machines, listening and viewing devices, and programmed books, complemented by optional encounter learning theory, team teaching, and tutors. Moreover, the possibilities for greater insights and advancing techniques portend opportunities for fantastic achievements in the future.

With this awareness, James Finn wrote, "It is my thesis that American education, considered as a culture in tradition, is now beginning the take-off stage into a high-order, high-energy culture, and that it is the first educational system in the world to reach this stage." (17)

Education, in reality, may become ecstasy. In *Education and Ecstasy*, George Leonard wrote,

> Men have always been willing to put their lives on the line for things that have seemed essential to their lives — food, water, salt, land, freedom from slavery, better wages and working conditions, racial equality. And now, behold: Education emerges as the most essential. . . . In the future a man's ability to learn and keep learning joyfully from birth to death will define the quality of life itself.

> . . . The [human condition] demands a new kind of human being — one who is not driven by narrow competition, eager acquisition and aggression, but who spends his life in the joyful pursuit of learning. Such a human being will result not as much through changed ideologies or economic systems as through changes in the process called "education." (18)

Summing Up

Your place of work is part of your choice of work: in capti-vating industry, big or small; in uncertain self-enterprise; in respected and responsible professionalism; or as a public ser-vant in government and teaching. Chances are that wherever you are, you will find elbow room for being inventive and ingenious.

For Exploration and Discussion

1. For more information on recruitment read *The Twenty Minute Lifetime* by Gavin A. Pitt (Englewood Cliffs, N.J.: Prentice-Hall Inc., 1957).

2. After reading *The Twenty Minute Lifetime*, write a résumé and present it to the class for criticism.

3. Investigate the most recent para-professional programs, includ-ing the MD assistant.

4. Visit an elementary school and discuss the teaching assistant program with a teacher.

5. With other members of the class, arrange and take a tour of your city and county government offices.

6. If you could change the work of the world, how would you change it? In your opinion, what work should be done by in-

dustry and what by government? Read Chapters 10 and 11 in the *Worldly Philosophers* by Robert Heilbronner (New York: Simon & Schuster, 1953).

7. What work needs desperately to be done? What is the relationship between work and racial disturbances? Research the problem to find some meaningful facts. The Department of Labor has some pertinent statistics on the employment of minority groups.

8. Read "The Coming Revolution in Transportation" by Frederick C. Appel, *National Geographic*, Washington, D.C., September 1969, pp. 301-341.

9. Investigate labor unions. Do you belong to one? Exchange experiences in class with those who do not belong. Read *Labor and the Public Interest* by Willard Wirtz (New York: Harper & Row, 1964), Chapters 4 and 5.

References

1. Edgar H. Schein, "The First Job Dilemma," *Psychology Today,* March, 1968, p. 28.

2. Schein, pp. 29-30.

3. H. N. Broom and J. G. Longenecker, *Small Business Management* (Chicago: Southwestern Publishing Company, 1966), p. 5.

4. *Occupational Outlook Handbook*, U. S. Department of Labor, Bureau of Labor Statistics (Washington, D.C.: Government Printing Office, 1966-67), p. 27.

5. John W. Macy Jr., "Federal Careers," *College Placement Annual* (Bethlehem, Pa.: College Placement Annual, Inc., 1968), p. 321.

6. Macy, p. 323.

7. *Careers in California State Government,* California State Personnel Board, Sacramento, 1969, (a) p. 11, (b) p. 10.

8. Michel Silva, "Big Government Wants You," *Careers Today,* January, 1969, p. 75.

9. William Macdonald, "Graduates Fiddle While City Hall Burns," *Careers Today*, January, 1969, p. 39.

10. John Tebbel, "People and Jobs," *Saturday Review*, December 30, 1967, p 10.

11. *Technical Education*. A report by the Commission on Science Education of the American Association for the Advancement of Science

(Washington, D.C.: American Association for the Advancement of Science Publications, 1968), p. 3.

12. *Technical Education*, p. 2-4.

13. *Twenty-Five Technical Careers You Can Learn in 2 Years or Less*, Department of Health, Education and Welfare (Washington, D.C.: Government Printing Office, 1971), pp. 3-4.

14. *Occupational Outlook Handbook*, p. 348.

15. Frank Riesman and Alan Gartner, "New Careers and Pupil Learning," *California Teachers Association Journal*, March, 1969, p. 9.

16. Jerome Bruner, "The New Educational Technology," *Revolution in Teaching* (New York: Bantam Books, 1964), p. 2.

17. Bruner, p. 27.

18. George Leonard, *Education and Ecstasy* (New York: Delacorte Press, 1968), pp. 217-230.

14

Changing Jobs

"Career choice is an art."

These electric words spring at me from a professional handbook I am reading. (1) Are they true? I weigh them against personal experience and professional theories, and must decide that like the practice of medicine, career choosing is truly an art.

What does such a statement mean to you? It means that you must rely on interpretation and, in some instances, intuition rather than precise mathematical formula to choose your career.

Before you are your tools: your intellect, your training, your talent, your strength, your spirit with its lively curiosity, and your commitment. Are you equal to choosing?

Again, startling words blaze at me from my book. "Whenever young people are given the necessary framework for their choices, I have found them to choose unerringly the work best suited to them."

So the choice is yours. You are the artist. "How does the artist begin?" you muse, not to me, but to yourself. "Not in a glorious sweep across the page, nor yet with a thundering crescendo." Your intuitive reply is true. The artist painstakingly blocks out his picture and then begins minutely to develop each fragment bit by bit. The musician grasps a tune, rewrites it, repeats it, elaborates; his score is on its way.

Your first job is probably behind you. Now, the choice is wider and the consequences more dramatic. Your awareness complicates an easy choice. You muster your inner forces, make a decision; you are now captive of a vital endeavor. Fear nags at your judgment. Quickly, you give yourself reassurance, "No job is forever." "A job is a job is a job." These reflections calm the panic of the crucial moment.

How long should you keep your job? Workers are becoming more mobile, with the average worker changing jobs at least six times within his working life. (2) The notable exception is the scientist. Many studies report that career choices in science are stable, often made when the chooser is in elementary school. In a study of the winners of the Science Talent Search, researchers found that 94 per cent of the winners continued in science. (3) Often, persons with exceptional talent quickly find their area of work. At the age of twenty, Arturo Toscanini became renowned almost overnight as a conductor and continued in this career for over fifty years. Not being geniuses, most of us must view what is possible and probable in the span of our working life.

The Three Stages of Work

An intensive analysis of job histories defined three stages of work for most workers: the *initial work period* consisting of the part time and full time jobs the individual holds until he completes his formal education; the *trial work period* when the individual experiments with jobs to find what he prefers; the *stable work period* when the worker remains on a job for three or more years. (4)

The Initial Stage

All the jobs, often quasi chores held before or after school, summer full time jobs, or a job taken only as a stop-gap until the completion of your education, are a part of the Initial Work Stage. "Occasionally, these become regular jobs, but as a rule they are temporary. The criterion is simply whether the job is held while the worker is pursuing his formal education. (5)

Often, college students receive some training or education in order to make a living while they continue their formal education. In one community college, a checker at Safeway Stores, a fireman, a vocational nurse, a computer programmer, and a library assistant are presently employed full time while enrolled in as many as 12 semester units in lower division courses required for a BA degree.

This initial work experience exposes you to innumerable opportunities to try different things and to observe whether you do them better or less well than others. Indirectly, these experiments guide you as you choose among the many activities that occupations offer.

The Trial Stage

The Trial Work Period is the stage of exploration in your choice of career. It may be that you will be satisfied with your first position, or you may be unable to find immediately the desired job, or further extensive training may be required. If you move from one occupation or place of work to another within a three year period you are considered in the trial work period. As Drucker suggested, it may be wise for you to change to another position, even one acknowledged to yourself as temporary, if it will further your sense of identity, purpose, and capability.

Properly researching any prospective job may be indicated. One company candidly informed an experimental group of recruiters about the disappointments and frustrations that were part of the work in their business. Recruitment of workers by this group resulted in a 33 per cent lower turnover in the first six months, a rate which continued for a two-year period. (6) A University of Texas professor berated students who work for an A in a trivial course and for the first job are not willing to extend an inch of time or energy to research what a company is like, who is there, or anything else about it. (7)

Changing jobs, like entering jobs successfully, depends upon acquiring the necessary information about the prospective job, combined with proper assessment of oneself in the present position.

....

Teacher to Police   A sixth grade teacher in an elementary school, John Terrill, recognizing the necessity in his city for more effective law enforcement, returned to college for police officer training. As a public relations man for the police department, he now visits schools in uniform to talk about the duties of the police force. In addition, he has initiated a plan whereby students, with parental permission, ride in a police car throughout a night while the officer explains what he is doing and why. This plan has been instituted throughout the city's high schools resulting in a dramatic decrease in campus incidents requiring police intervention and eliminating youthful gang warfare. Terrill's experience in his first trial job led to the new job, now a stable and rewarding career.

....

In a twenty-seven year follow-up on job satisfaction, Robert Hoppock found that the greatest increase in job satisfaction was achieved by those who changed jobs. In fact, the worker with the least job satisfaction was an English teacher who taught English during a thirty year period. (8)

The Stable Stage

The Stable Work Period is the stage during which a worker remains in a given occupation and place of work for three years or more, holding a relatively permanent job and establishing some social roots both at work and in the community. This period may occur, disappear, and then reoccur during the life of the worker. As you would expect, certain occupations are more stable than others; workers who enter them generally remain for several years. When occupations are ranked from most stable to least stable, according to the number of years workers habitually remain in them, workers rank in this order: first, professionals; second, proprietors and managers; third, clerical; fourth, skilled; then a big dip to the fifth, semi-skilled; sixth, unskilled; and seventh, domestic and personal help. The least stable, taxi-drivers, waiters, filling station attendants, janitors, and farm laborers may never have a job that lasts for three years. (9)

Another way to look at occupations is to observe the number of years spent in the Initial and Trial Periods before the worker moves into the Stable Period. Professionals and semiprofessional workers who generally struggle to establish themselves, spend approximately four years in the Initial Period, four years in the Trial Period and eighteen years in the Stable Period, during which they may hold three jobs. In all classifications, the average was three years in the Initial Period, six years in the Trial Period, and eighteen years in the Stable Period. Semi-skilled and unskilled workers, however, spent many more years in the Initial and Trial Periods. (10)

Work Mobility

When a change of job occurs at the same occupational level it is called *horizontal mobility*; when a job changes into a more rewarding occupational level (in income, prestige, or power), it is referred to as *vertical mobility*.

Through study of job histories of workers one may discover the character and amount of mobility occurring at each occupational level. An intensive study of a large group of workers revealed these trends:

1. Professional workers started their initial work on many different levels but once they became professionals only a few tried other work. Those that did usually took positions as proprietors or managers.
2. Proprietors, managers, and officials showed much vertical movement in the Initial and Trial Periods before entering the Stable Period.
3. Clerical workers exhibited some vertical movement before reaching the clerical level but little after that.
4. The patterns for the skilled workers and foremen indicated that they began their work as unskilled and semi-skilled

labor. When they became skilled workers and foremen, they achieved a high degree of stability.

5. The semi-skilled workers displayed some vertical movement, for many of them had early jobs as personal and domestic service workers. Mobility above the semi-skilled level, once it was attained, was infrequent.

6. Many workers in unskilled and domestic service jobs remained at the original classification; they experienced many trial jobs and only fleeting security. (11)

During any work period, movement may be horizontal when the worker searches for a more suitable environment in which to work at the same job. The skilled worker may watch for an opportunity to be placed with a well known company that has extensive fringe benefits. The office worker may move to more comfortable surroundings and pleasant working relationships. A nurse in a small town hospital may apply for a position in a city hospital. In many school districts, teachers who are hired latest are placed in the least desired schools (according to discipline, moral acceptability and teachability) and from there, after some service, may request to be moved to a more desirable school. In teaching, movement also may be from one grade or instructional level to another, from one subject to another, or from teaching to counseling, or both.

Career Patterns

When analyzing work histories, researchers often find an orderly movement, either horizontally or vertically, from one job to another, that forms a *career pattern*. Among several basic types of career patterns, each individual's work history would probably deviate to some extent. Four career patterns can be identified: extrinsic, coherent, intrinsic, and erratic.

The *extrinsic career pattern* is one in which the worker moves to increasingly more responsible work within an occupation. One extrinsic pattern is part of the nature of the work itself. The worker moves vertically from one skill to a more advanced one; the file clerk may go smoothly into typing, to office machines, and from there to secretarial work. Similarly, the data processor may move to computer programmer. And the college instructor is promoted to assistant, to associate, and then to full professor.

Some companies take responsibility for the extrinsic career pattern. They hire the worker in a basic entry job, then shift him upward into a variety of positions until he appears to reach his potential.

....

Sandy   Sandy started selling in the sweater shop of a large department store. Suddenly she was moved to housewares, then yardage. One year later, she was selling in one of the most difficult departments, draperies, being trained to become the assistant interior decorator.

....

Salesmen may be said to have extrinsic career patterns when they move from selling kitchenware, to books, to automobiles, to real estate, and to insurance.

The *coherent career pattern* involves a series of vertical job moves which are only loosely related to form a pattern. The teacher may become a supervisor, then a principal; the saleswoman becomes a buyer, model, or interior decorator; and the skilled worker moves to be a foreman or a union leader.

....

The Political Barber   One ambitious young barber first moved to shop ownership; from there, he specialized in men's hair design. Because of his involvement in the licensing program, he was asked to teach two courses in apprentice barbering. When his students did remarkably well in the state examinations, he was invited to sit on the State Apprenticeship Board. This he did not accept for several reasons, but he did become a legislative advocate. This unique career pattern emerged because of his fine speaking ability and his intense interest in people, but all his activities centered around his basic career choice, barbering.

....

The *intrinsic career pattern* evolves from the increasing development of unusual talent or commitment within the worker. The Peace Corps worker may move to social case work or community work. Ansel Adams, world renowned photographer, was once a concert pianist who was moved by the beauty of Yosemite National Park to spend his life trying to capture it on film.

With a fine mixture of humor and satire, John Ciardi, the poet, writes of his career pattern.

....

John Ciardi   I will do anything for money. Anything, that is, but work for it. Work is too good a thing to do for money. Work, to be sure, may produce pay checks. I cannot doubt that T. S. Eliot, though he incidentally died a millionaire, wrote for the doing of it, accepting the bonuses as pleasurable happenstances. . . . [However,] any man who made the original blunder of choosing low income parents is likely to be drawn to some employment. If he is lucky enough, or wise enough, or both together, his employment will be his work: he will find a way to earn his living doing exactly what he would like to do if he had no living to earn. . . . It would follow down-scale from him, that a man is happy, or at least lucky, to the degree that he keeps his work up and his employment down.

What I work at is my desk. Unfortunately my work leaves me in need of some employment. In less fruitful days I was employed for nine months of each year as an English professor waiting for the three summer months in which I could get back to work. Then I discovered the lecture circuit. As an underpaid professor, my employment to work stint was 9 to 3. I resigned my job seven years ago and instantly found myself so joyously overpaid in the lecture circuit that I could reverse the ratio of work to employment and still have seven or eight times more money.

That I am in fact overpaid is not a brag but a gladness. It is also a statement of fact. No man is worth what I get paid for an hour's talk—a poet who speaks only off the top of his head. The world is mad to pay such fees, but I would be madder yet to argue. . . . The fact is that the higher the fees go, the less lecture circuit employment I need take on, and the sooner I can get back to work. I don't want it all. I just want what I want fast enough to stop needing more soonest. (12)

....

Ralph Nader   Ralph Nader's career pattern is somewhat like John Ciardi's. About twenty times a year, he lectures to raise money to live on, so that he can work at what he enjoys. With his work and leisure totally integrated, he works day and night. "I happen to like what I do very much," he explains. "I actually find that the act of staying up till dawn researching a confidential memorandum is pleasurable. It's just that I would rather work 20 hours a day on something that gives me real satisfaction than three hours a day on an alienating job that bores me."

Mr. Nader earned $60,000 from his book *Unsafe at Any Speed*, but spent it to finance new investigations. While a method of support, his speeches also add to his influence on the public, making consumers aware of their neglected interests. A lawyer by profession, he became a lawyer for the people and, in turn, a director of other professionals who united also to become lawyers in the interest of the public. (13)

....

An *erratic career pattern* is found most often among unskilled workers who move from one job to another with no continuity. This career pattern is the most unstable and accounts for much of the unemployment and underemployed. The movement here should focus on movement upward through training.

This unfortunate career pattern occurs also when a worker after a decade of work is filled with despair by the realities of his working life. This pattern is strongly documented in the studies of the California Institute of Technology where the assistant director of the Industrial Relations Center, Lee Stockford, has studied more than 4,000 men and women employed in large industries. His studies provide evidence of the disillusionment workers may feel around their mid-thirties when they suddenly become aware that their ideals and dreams have faded and that their lives are mundane. According to Stockford, in a corporation of 1,000 employees, 39 will be vocationally dislocated and 350 will become disillusioned and quit. He believes that changing jobs may help; it depends on whether the individual is running away from a situation that repels him or running to something that will be more satisfying. With time, a majority of people work their way through the malaise and recover their job morale. It is a reality gap, the gap between the realities of life and the idealistic expectations of younger people, that Stockford believes is responsible for the "over 30" despair. (14)

The New Job

More and more evidence is accumulating to help you find the job you really want. The traditional ways you probably know: the State Employment Agency, College Placement, private agencies, the newspapers, personnel offices, and recruiters. Perhaps you have been coached on writing résumés or making interviews. All of these methods which you may have used before can be useful in obtaining a new position. What seems to have been overlooked in the past, however, is the fact that more people get jobs through friends or acquaintances than any other way.

Think again of Shapero's study of 3,000 scientists and engineers. He discovered that 51 per cent of them first heard about their jobs through friends and a full two-thirds found their jobs without going through the normal recruiting channels. The human grapevine, he believes, is the best way to get a job. (15) It is understandable that a friend in the company you want to work for can be invaluable because the company realizes that the friend's reputation will be tied to your performance. Recently, a college Dean said, "I've made up my mind not to hire another faculty member unless someone on the staff knows him." For the employer, too, the personal recruiter is beneficial.

An occupational contact network does exist. (16) This phenomenon is the practice of keeping in touch with persons with whom you have worked. The contact may be slight—a Christmas card, a telephone call, a vacation remembrance, or a chance meeting at some event. You may not be close friends or even had close working relations, but informal contact does occur. As fellow workers move throughout the area or even the nation, they create a network of contacts available to their friends. When an individual is seeking a new job, he does not write the personnel manager or make the distant trip; he writes or calls his former colleague, to learn from him the working conditions, the bosses, and where the vacancies exist.

A company of a thousand workers which moved from the West Coast to the East took with them the few workers who wished to go. For two years, the colleagues who remained checked with each other to find who liked his job or who needed to change, and to offer suggestions or give tips and recommendations.

Fruit packers and migratory workers also have elaborate mechanisms for assuring that their own friends will be hired by a particular boss. When the best location for work is known, one person often goes ahead and makes arrangements for his friends to work there. Friends, relatives, acquaintances, former co-workers, or a friend of a friend-of-a-friend are all part of your resources in finding the job you want.

Changing jobs may be the most crucial and challenging aspect of your entire working life. To demand the best of yourself and to be courageous in the face of anxiety and uncertainty are noble and necessary aims. The finest words of encouragement were those spoken by William Faulkner when he accepted the Nobel Prize for Literature in Stockholm, December 10, 1950.*

> I feel that this award was not made to me as a man, but to my work—a life work in the agony and sweat of the human spirit, not for glory and least of all for profit, but to create out of the materials of the human spirit something which did not exist before.
>
> (Man) must teach himself that the basest of all things is to be afraid; and, teaching himself that, forget it forever, leaving no room in his workshop for anything but the old verities and truths of the heart. . . . love and honor and pity and pride and compassion and sacrifice. Until he does so, he labors under a curse.
>
> . . . I decline to accept the end of man. It is easy enough to say that man is immortal simply because he will endure: that when the last ding-dong of doom has clanged and faded from the last worthless rock hanging tideless in the last red and dying evening, that even then there will be one more sound: that of his puny inexhaustible voice, still talking. I refuse to accept this. I believe that man will not merely endure: he will prevail. He is immortal, not because he alone among creatures has an inexhaustible voice, but because he

has a soul, a spirit capable of compassion and sacrifice and endurance...." (17)

For Exploration and Discussion

1. "Vocational decision should be viewed as a process, not an event." Defend this statement.

2. Discuss with members of the class, relatives, or adults you know, their experiences in changing jobs and finally reaching their present job status. Include in your interrogation persons whose careers you admire.

3. In *The Sociology of Work*, Theodore Caplow presents a study of those social roles which arise from the classification of men by the work they do. Scan this work and read as much of it as you choose. (Minneapolis: Minnesota Press, 1954).

4. Exchange information with members of the class of novels that portray a vivid picture of the reality of certain kinds of work, for example:
   Bel Kaufman, *Up the Down Staircase* (Englewood Cliffs: Prentice-Hall, 1964).
   Jonathan Kozol, *Death at an Early Age* (New York: Bantam Books, 1968).
   Both of the above books illuminate teaching the disadvantaged. James Hilton, *Goodbye, Mr. Chips* (Boston: Little, Brown & Co., 1934) captures teaching the young advantaged school boy. Alice Hobart, *Oil for the Lamps of China* (Indianapolis: Bobbs Merrill, 1933) depicts the frustrations and hopes of an ambitious junior executive.

Sloan Wilson, *Man in the Gray Flannel Suit* (New York: Simon Schuster, 1955) epitomizes the values of the aspiring business man.

Arthur Hailey, *Airport* (Garden City, N.Y.: Doubleday, 1968) depicts realistically the work life at an airport.

References

1. Max Baer and Edward Roehr, *Occupational Information* (Chicago: Science Research Associates Inc., 1964), p. 179.

2. *Occupational Outlook Handbook* (Washington, D.C.: Government Printing Office, 1966-67), p. 18.

3. Robert Hoppock, *Occupational Information* (New York: McGraw-Hill, 1967), p. 99.

4. William H. Form and Delbert Miller, "Occupational Career Pattern as a Sociological Instrument," Sigmund Nosow and William Form, eds. *Man, Work and Society*, (New York: Basic Books, Inc., 1962), p. 288.

5. Form and Miller, p. 288.

6. Hoppock, p. 382.

7. Gay Boyer, "College (Dis)Placement Offices," *Careers Today,* March 1969, p. 82.

8. Robert Hoppock, "A Twenty-seven Year Follow-up on Job Satisfaction of Employed Adults, *Personnel and Guidance Journal*, February 1960, p. 489.

9. Form and Miller, p. 290.

10. Form and Miller, p. 290.

11. Form and Miller, p. 292.

12. John Ciardi, "Manner of Speaking," *Saturday Review*, November 16, 1968, p. 20. © 1968 Saturday Review, Inc.

13. Jack Newfield, "Nader's Raiders," *Life Magazine*, October 3, 1969, pp. 56-63.

14. Gay Boyer, "Over 30 Despair: the Reality Gap," *Careers Today,* February 1969, p. 68.

15. Boyer, "College (Dis) Placement Offices," p. 84.

16. Fred Katz, "Occupational Contact Netwworks," Nosow and Form, eds, *Man, Work and Society*, pp. 317-321.

17. William Faulkner, *The Faulkner Reader* (New York: Random House, Inc., 1954).

15

Choosing Again

Choosing a part time job in retirement, lessening or changing the duties of work as one grows older, seems to have been an arrangement developed by primitive man.

One writer describes the aging process in a primitive society:

> Old people who were past the prime of life did not remain in idleness, but occupied themselves in work requiring no great expenditure of energy. Old women plaited baskets and aged persons of both sexes made twine and cordage of all kinds for nets and snares. Besides grinding and fitting stone implements, old men spent much time in rubbing down greenstone into adzes and ornaments. Such work was monotonous, but not heavy; it gave them occupation, soothed their nerves, and had this advantage that they could cease and begin again whenever they felt so inclined. (1)

Now, with a longer life expectancy, a higher standard of living, better food, and increased medical care, man can work more productively during a longer work life.

Productivity of the Older Worker

Several studies on the productivity and performance of older workers have been made by the National Association of Manufacturers, the Bureau of National Affairs, Factory Management and Maintenance, and the Bureau of Employment Security. Conclusions are that older workers are as good as, and sometimes better than, the younger workers in overall performance; that in eight or nine cases out of ten, the employer rates the older worker (including workers 60 and over) as capable or more capable than his younger workers; and finally, that two-fifths or more of the older workers exceed the production norms of the entire work force being studied. (2) Generally the older person must exert more imaginative initiative to find work than the younger individual.

Placement of the Older Worker

More attention is now being given to the assets which the older worker has to offer. Juvenal Angel, Director of the Modern Vocational Trade Bureau, has said: The assets of mature workers, both men and women, include fewer industrial accidents, less job shifting, a keen sense of loyalty, stability, and a greater sense of responsibility. When muscular strength and speed do not count in job performance, mature workers get better results than younger workers. (3)

Angel completed a thorough study of the mature worker and his occupational problems and opportunities. He suggests that self-analysis, resumé writing, assessment of positions, interviewing, and knowing why older people sometimes fail to get jobs can be helpful in choosing again. Analyzing positions for men and women according to occupational aptitudes and functions, he classified over 500 positions into 28 major groups, with the occupational titles, requirements, and personal characteristics required. Groups listed include "Positions for those who have proven ability to lead," "Positions for those who are 'idea' men or women," "Positions for those who like the outdoor life," "Positions for those who can shoulder responsibility," "Positions for those who are mathematically minded," "Positions for those who like being on the move," and over twenty others. (4)

The middle-aged or older worker should not feel that he must struggle alone to find a new position; rather, it will be to his advantage to seek assistance through the employment service. Recent studies proved that after receiving employment counseling, more than twice as many mature workers were placed, or found jobs on their own, as those who did not have these services. (5) It is possible that the need to find employment during the middle years may be the first opportunity a worker has had actually to choose a career, since he may have taken a position as a young person through a trial and error method, or without understanding his own nature or abilities. If this is true, it is another reason for making the search for a new position a thorough, well-planned and careful process.

The Need for a Change

It is not unusual for a man who has worked for twenty or thirty years to want a complete change of work. The chances are that the more abilities, interests, and imagination that he has, the more apt he is to need variety in his working life.

....

Sergeant-Teacher   At one city college, a mathematics professor is a graduate of West Point. After twenty years in the armed services, he retired as a Colonel, ready and enthusiastic for a new career in teaching. In one of his classes is an ex-master sergeant who completed his twentieth year in the armed forces as director of aerial photography in the Far East. "I really liked my job," the sergeant confessed, "but my wife and children want me to stay home. Since I've worked a great deal with young people, I think I'd like to teach."

....

More and more, mothers whose youngest children have at last enrolled in school, look for a job outside the home. Having established their husbands in satisfying careers they look for fulfillment for themselves in outside employment.

In most careers, there doubtless are some points at which changing to another career is relatively easy, and it is possible that the skills and information gained in any career may open new opportunities for others.

Career Change and Uncertainty

Apprehension is a part of most career changes. For the older worker, as mentioned previously, new positions are not as easily found as for the younger person. Undoubtedly this deters many persons who otherwise would make the drastic move. Discontent with doing the same thing, or nearly the same thing, for many years within one company can start the middle-aged executive daydreaming about a second career based on same latent aptitude or a favorite college course. Generally, he does nothing about it, according to surveys that have been made. (6) The realization that he would be abandoning his present skills for untried demands often makes it seem too risky for him to venture the change. Some graduate schools are attempting to assist successful workers who want to make a change and who are willing to take at least a minimum risk.

A New Careers program at Columbia University's School of General Studies for men and women between the ages of 35 and 50 attracted over 4,500 letters of inquiry in two years. Other universities report sales managers studying to be botanists, lawyers turning to geology, and mechanical engineers taking up law. At Columbia, a reporter interviewed one of the new career men.

....

New Career Man   E. King Graves was a sales and advertising executive for an industrial packaging company who found his job becoming a strenuous rat race. He had always enjoyed working with his hands and his hobby for many years had been making furniture in a woodworking shop at his home in Cold Spring Harbor in Long Island. When one of his sons suggested that he could become a manual training teacher, Graves resigned from his sales job and started a new life studying industrial arts instruction at City College in New York under a Ford Foundation grant. Now he is teaching mechanical shop work, ceramics, and graphic arts to deaf children at P.S. 47, the School for the Deaf in New York. From his statements, at 60 years old, he is finding a satisfaction and a feeling of accomplishment he never before knew. (7)

A realistic approach to making a career change by an older individual is to enroll in training at a local community college or four year college.

In the fall of 1970, 500 persons over thirty years of age and 45 persons over fifty years of age enrolled at San Jose City College. Although apprehensive at first about their ability to succeed and to be accepted by younger students, these older individuals found themselves enjoying their associations and challenged by the excitement of learning.

Counselor   Enrolled at the community college was a man of 45 who had worked in the county sheriff's department for twenty years before suffering a heart attack. Warned by the doctor that he must change his occupation, Mr. Mabane explored the possibility of working as a counselor for youths in the Juvenile Detention Home. Because he was a warm, friendly person who had been particularly concerned with young people in his former job, and who related well with the young college students, his college counselor encouraged him in his tentative choice. A year later he was enthusiastic about his college studies and satisfied with his choice of a new career.

Librarian   Mrs. Jacobs felt useless and left out when the members of her family scattered for the day's activities. With an excellent record in her one year of college work, taken twenty years before, she enrolled in college and selected the course for training as a library technician. During her internship, she was recommended to substitute in a university library. There her responsible and competent performance resulted in an offer of a permanent position. At present, in addition to her work at the university, she is continuing her studies to become a fully certificated librarian.

She explains that a highlight in her life was her graduation from the community college with an AA degree because that same month her daughter graduated from the State College with a BA degree and her son received his diploma from the local high school.

Social Welfare Worker   Mrs. Moody wished to enroll in the program for registered nurses but she had difficulty in passing the required science courses. For over a year she continued taking courses in the liberal arts program hoping that this foundation would prepare her for satisfactory work in the sciences. When her husband became chronically ill, Mrs. Moody was forced to look for work. She took the Civil Service Examination and because of her recent background in college studies performed well on the test resulting in an offer of a position as a social worker. "This was really what I wanted and didn't realize it," she explained. "Working with people in a very personal way was what attracted me to nursing."

Opportunities for change are more readily available than most people realize. In the words of Seymour Wolfbein, there is a developing commitment "to use all the instruments of manpower policy to sustain a level of education opportunities for all who wish and seek them; from Head Start to the Higher Education Facilities Act, from on-the-job training in the private sector to the millions of company-supported classroom hours of instruction with pay to its employees by industry and

business." (8) Moreover, the adult education program and the extended day curriculum of the community colleges attract every weekday night large numbers of mature workers, many of them seeking new ways to change their employment.

The changing world of work will not only facilitate changes in employment but may require them. With the new opportunities for education and for work experience, the adult worker, too, may realize within himself an enlarging sense of identity.

For Exploration and Discussion

1. In the library, find some publications on the employment of older workers, scanning them for their usefulness; then report to the class on the ones you found most valuable.

2. Observe older people employed in businesses, institutions and industries which you contact. Do they appear to be happy, contented, capable, reliable? If possible, talk with some of them about their work.

3. Interview a personnel man in a working establishment or an employment agency to determine the employment possibilities and problems of older workers in your community.

4. Discuss the contributions that older men and women have made to society. In which occupations are they usually found?

5. Invite an elderly worker to the class to talk about his (or her) career. With his permission, have members of the class ask numerous questions concerning his satisfactions and dissatisfactions, challenges and hopes.

6. Discuss with the registrar the number of older men and women enrolled in your college. If there are older persons enrolled in your classes, become acquainted and discover their goals.

7. Angel includes a bibliography of over 100 publications, each concerned primarily with the employment of the mature person and having such titles as these:

    M.C. Briggs, *400 Jobs for People Over 60*

    Massachusetts Department of Labor and Industries, *How the Mature Worker Finds His Job*

Ed Kohn, *Job Opportunities for Older People*
E. T. Breckenbridge, *Effective Use of Older Workers*
Find and scan one or two of these books. Discuss your findings with other students and with some older friends who are working.

References

1. Raymond Firth, *Primitive Economics of the New England Maori* (New York: E. P. Dutton & Company, 1929), p. 200.

2. Charles E. Odell, "Productivity of the Older Worker," *Vocational Guidance and Career Development*, Herman J. Peters and James C. Hansen, eds. (New York: Macmillan, 1966), p. 457.

3. Juvenal Angel, *Occupations for Men and Women after 45*, 3rd ed. (New York: World Trade Academy Press, Inc., 1964), p. 3.

4. Angel, pp. 33-57.

5. Angel, p. 169.

6. D. A. Saunders, "Executive Discontent," *Man, Work and Society*, Sigmund Nosow and William Form, eds. (New York: Basic Books Inc., 1962), pp. 466-467.

7. "People in Action," *This Week Magazine*, March 15, 1966, pp. 6, 7.

8. Seymour Wolfbein, *Occupational Information* (New York: Random House, 1968), p. 142.

16

The Workman's Progress

Since each person is unique, no two persons will experience the same working situation. Your work life will be your own.

You may have found the direction for your work life or you still may be uncertain of your choice of work and feel apprehensive. Again, remember that each individual develops with a unique timetable. If you are learning more about the areas of work and your personal preferences and abilities for work, at some time you will be able to choose wisely. Further education may be a requirement before you can make a career decision.

....

The Dean   A young college dean explained his dilemma to a group of students. "As a high school graduate," he said, "I never expected to go on to college, but I applied for a scholarship because my friends were applying. To my surprise I received a scholarship to a large university miles away from my home town. There I suffered for two years. Each semester I was homesick. My professors were impersonal; the courses were difficult and the grading was severe. Each semester I was ready to give up and go home. Somehow I held on until my junior year when I gradually realized what I was studying for; then I began to enjoy school."

The students who listened spoke of their identity with the dean's dilemma, "holding on " until the goal was clear.

....

You will live your work life in the decades of a century that will reveal the now unforeseeable future. To live your work life successfully you will need the same attributes as you do for a successful personal life. You must live in the *now* with an eye for the *future.* As you persist in a job, you will develop self-confidence which in return will enable you to seek and accept new opportunities. In this manner, you will progress throughout your working life.

Unemployment

Like Christian in *Pilgrims Progress* on his way to the Celestial City, you may meet some difficulties. One of these is unemployment. The rapid changes taking place in the country as it adjusts to a peace time economy and at the same time absorbs the latest technology undoubtedly will create lags and gaps in worker demands. You may be one of those who is "displaced."

The problem is not that your work is not needed. There will be expanding material needs for a population that is centered on the age group of 21—35 years until 1980. In addition, the important issues of this decade—the environment, urban centers, health care, racial opportunities, transportation, and recreation—need vast talent and trained manpower. Then, why unemployment? One economic analyst explained that every additional skilled or educated worker requires a prior investment of at least $20,000 in new capital. (1) To acquire the capital and to invest it advantageously takes time and expertise.

The Department of Labor is aware of the unemployment potential and is seeking to control it. Secretary of Labor James D. Hodgsen under the Nixon administration said, "The nation's manpower future is shaped by tens of millions of individual decisions by employers, students, workers, union officials, educators, and government officials. Our aim is to provide all of them with clear and meaningful information that will enable them to act wisely and promptly". (2)

If you are faced with unemployment, what should you do? Each individual must find his own answers, but here are some suggestions from persons who have faced this eventuality:

1. Maintain your self-respect. It is not a personal indictment to be unemployed but a phase of the time in which you live. With cheerfulness, bravado, or discipline, survey the economic situation in your community.

2. Resort to all known techniques for obtaining a job as detailed in Chapter 13.

3. Apply at the nearest U.S.E.S. Job Bank, a computer center that matches job seekers with jobs, to determine if there is an appropriate job for you in another part of the country.

4. Maintain a routine of self-improvement: improve your physical appearance, keep informed with current reading, enroll in interesting adult education courses.

5. Talk with officials at the nearest local Cooperative Manpower Planning System Committee (CAMPS) to explore the possibility of further training for new kinds of jobs. The committee may recommend a government organization called New Careers for your appraisal.

6. If you feel yourself filled with despair, take a trip. Visit friends in another part of the state, go camping, for a short time change your environment. This will boost your morale.

7. Be creative and inventive. Look around you for whatever you can make or do that someone will appreciate. Bake flavorful bread; grow flowers and vegetables; get involved in photography; build picture frames; organize a band; groom, train, and exercise dogs; collect butterflies or river rock; search for rare books, stamps, or coins.

8. If you see a need, fill it whether or not you are paid adequately. Volunteer work will help you main-

tain your dignity and may lead to an employment opportunity.

Many persons have made themselves indispensible and thus established themselves in a job.

....

The Indispensible Therapist   Caroline, a speech pathologist, worked for two years with no salary and the third year for token pay in order to establish a much needed child center for language handicapped children. A medical school, the grateful parents, and a considerate husband encouraged the project. When the children entered public school, their good adjustment was so evident that the county allotted a substantial sum of money to maintain the school and to pay Caroline and the other speech therapists adequate salaries.

....

The Dietitian   A home economics major without employment took a position during the evening hours at a rest home. When her casual suggestions concerning the food and other management problems proved valuable, she was asked to replace the managing supervisor who was moving to another state.

....

The Dramatist   A drama major worked nights in a factory to enable him to work during the day with junior high school students in a theatre group producing plays for the children of the community. Two years later he was appointed the first salaried recreation leader in the community. Later, he was promoted to manager of the civic auditorium and assistant in the city's cultural affairs.

....

When your goal is to fill a need and to keep active, you may discover work you can do.

Misdirection

In addition to unemployment, another difficulty you may encounter as you progress in your work life is misjudging a job you accept. Misjudgment may be caused by a lack of understanding of what the job demands or else by lack of experience in what the activity involves.

An efficiency expert in a placement office described some changes that were made within one's company:

....

New Directions   An average supply inspector who liked people better than he liked materials was placed in the personnel office where he performed well. A clerk whose position was about to be terminated had above average intelligence but was unable to use it on the job and had become bored. She was transferred to a more responsible job where she worked successfully. On the other hand, a superior filing clerk was made a supervisor. Shortly after her promotion, the company received resignation notices. As a supervisor she was out of her element.

....

Youth Leader   A successful youth leader of a church was appointed the head minister of an adult congregation of another church. In the new position he needed executive and managerial ability in business affairs, visiting time for the aged of his parish, and the ability to devise and deliver fluent, if not eloquent, sermons. None of these requirements were part of his former position. After three years of trial and error, by mutual consent, he relinquished his pastorate. Once again involved primarily with youth in a close relationship, now he is content in his work.

....

Vocational Life Stages

Your work life will progress through developmental stages. (3) Already, you have experienced some of them: As an infant you learned to trust people and be aware of your world; as a child you learned to assert yourself and to play at work; in school you tested yourself against your peers and dreamed of *fantasy* jobs such as a T.V. star, ballplayer, or pilot. As a teenager, you asked yourself, "Of all the things I can do, what do I choose to do?" And you got your first job and sensed the heady, excruciating experience of independence.

Your first *tentative* choices of jobs enabled you to make more *realistic* ones.

With a realistic choice of work you now are ready to invest your time and energy in your chosen field. While you involve yourself in life, perhaps with marriage and children, you will commit yourself also to mastery and advancement in your work.

Before you are two other stages of vocational life: the mature worker and the retired worker. The mature worker seeks a community role. (4) At the peak of his occupational career he often accepts civic responsibility and shifts his emphasis from individual gain to social betterment, enriching his life with varying types of activity. The retired worker looks back over his life of work, contemplates his successes and failures and accepts within himself his social contribution, finding in the things and people he enjoys a satisfying relationship to the world.

See Table 10 for an extension of the developmental stages, described by psychologists, sociologists, philosophers, and vocational counselors. (5)

No career choice is final and not until late in his career will the average man be able to sum up his total expectations with some degree of finality. (6)

Vocational Success

The criterion for vocational success will have to be your own. Many of your generation have displayed attitudes of service such as human responsibility, respect, and altruism. A group of young doctors announced their policy of giving every young person in the county 18 years of age or younger a free physical examination and established office hours for this purpose certain evenings each week. With this same spirit, young people are joining Vista and the Peace Corps.

An authority on young people, Kenneth Kenniston, wrote that to today's youth knowledge that does not grow out of or

Table 10 Developmental Stages of Man and His Work (5)

Physical Development	Erickson's Developmental Tasks	Relationships	Vocational Question	Work Role	Occupational Choices	Job Involvement
Childhood	Basic trust Autonomy Initiative Industry	I — It	Am I? Who am I? What can I do?	Growth	Fantasy choices	Preparatory play
Adolescence	Identity	Thou	What will I do?	Exploration	Tentative choices	Initial jobs Trial jobs
Maturity	Intimacy Genealogy Integrity	I — Thou	What meaning does what I do have for me?	Establishment Maintenance	Realistic choices	Stable jobs Retirement

feed back into personal experience and action hardly seems worth knowing, that above the objective and scientific are the personally relevant, immediate, and experiental.

You may recognize your goals among the goals referring to life work that Kenniston presents:

1. *New forms of adulthood* in which . . . the betterment of society can be continued in adult work that does not require blind acceptance of the established System, but permits continuing commitment to social change . . .
2. *A new orientation to the future* that avoids the fixed tasks and defined life works of the past in favor of an openness and acceptance of flux and uncertainty . . .
3. *New pathways of personal development* wherein openness, fluidity, growth, and change, the responsiveness to inner life and historical need can be maintained throughout life.
4. *New value for living* that will fill the spiritual emptiness created by material affluence.
5. *New types of social organization*, institutional forms that include rather than exclude . . . "that will activate, harmonize, and strengthen those they touch."

Kenniston sums up these goals in this way, "However we judge the young radicals, to describe their search is to enumerate the problems of our changing, affluent and violent society, ..." (7)

In a similar commitment to finding values worthy of mankind, over one hundred years ago an American writer explored the choices with his heroes. Nathaniel Hawthorne, admittedly a romantic who wrote the first great American novel, was a teller of tales based on the myths that swirled about his New England town where he quietly taught himself to write. A puritan at heart, Hawthorne saw in life what he perceived to be man's constant moral decision in choosing right against wrong. His short story, *The Great Stone Face*, reads like a parable of career choice.

Ernest grew up in the shadow of the man shaped in the mountains, aware of the prophecy that some day someone from his small valley would be acclaimed for his greatness and he would possess the visage of the Great Stone Face.

First to be hailed was Mr. Gathergold who had amassed a fortune with his merchant ships and who the villagers said had a perfect, undeniable similitude to the Man of the Mountain. Deeply stirred, Ernest awaited his appearance only to see an old man with wizened yellow skin and piercing, squinting eyes, from whom he turned quickly away.

Then came Old Blood and Thunder, an illustrious commander who "had the same face to a hair as the Great Stone Face and he was undoubtedly the greatest man of the age." In him Ernest beheld a war worn and weathered countenance, full of energy and expressions of an iron will, but the gentle wisdom and deep, tender sympathies were altogether lacking in his face and Ernest admitted to himself that he was not the man of prophecy.

Next came the politician who had garnered the name Old Stony Phiz for political advantage, truly a man of eloquence but about him Ernest saw unmistakably a weary gloom.

The years swept by and Ernest, whitehaired and wrinkled, learned of a poet, a man of genius, whose songs seemed worthy of the greatness he saw in the Great Stone Face. It happened that the poet heard of Ernest and of his character and the noble simplicity of his life for Ernest had become a leader through his wise counsel and his genuine concern for the welfare of others. The poet came to visit him and looking at Ernest he asked, "Why are you sad?" "Because," replied Ernest, "all through life I have awaited the fulfillment of a prophecy and when I read the poems I hoped that it would be fulfilled in you."

"You hoped," answered the poet, "to find in me the likeness of the Great Stone Face. But my life, Ernest, has not corresponded with my thoughts. I have had great dreams but I lacked faith in the grandeur, the beauty, the goodness which my own words declare." The poet spoke sadly.

At evening, when the villagers gathered to hear the poet read, Ernest rose to introduce him. At a distance, but distinctly to be seen, high up in the golden light of the setting sun, appeared the Great Stone Face with hoary mist around it, like the white hair around the brow of Ernest. At this the poet arose and impulsively cried aloud, "Behold! Behold! Ernest is himself the likeness of the Great Stone Face."

> "Before you is set Life and Death
> "Therefore, choose Life." (8)

It is the underlying assumption of this text that man does have a choice of work delineated by his experience and learning, and culminating in emerging opportunities for new choice throughout his lifetime.

For Exploration and Discussion

1. Read in Erik Erickson's *Childhood and Society* (New York: W. W. Norton & Company, 1963), Chapter 7, "Eight Ages of Man." Discuss with your group the relationship of this developmental concept to your own growth or the development of persons you knew well. Attempt to answer the question, "Do I see myself as others see me?"

2. Define the meaning of integrity to a person who is handicapped or deprived or the victim of discrimination.

3. Relate the philosophy of the "Now Generation" to the vocational and developmental process.

4. Present to the class a book review highlighting the developmental phases of a significant character in the book.

5. Share your own vocational aspirations and present vocational development with the group.

References

1. Peter F. Drucker, "The Surprising Seventies," *Harper's Magazine*, July, 1971, p. 38.

2. James D. Hodgson, *Orbit*, Department of Labor Bulletin, December 1, 1970, p. 1.

3. David B. Hershenson, "Life-Stage Vocational Development System," *The Psychology of Vocational Development,* Roth, Hershenson, and Hilliard, eds. (Boston: Allyn & Bacon, Inc., 1970), pp. 110-119. Erik Erickson, *Childhood and Society* (New York: W. W. Norton, Inc. 1963), pp. 247-274.

4. Robert Havighurst, "Youth in Exploration and Man Emergent," *Man in a World of Work,* Henry Borow, ed. (Boston: Houghton Mifflin Company, 1964), p. 216.

5. Based on the research and writings of Erik Erickson, Eli Ginzberg, Donald Super, David Hershenson, and Joseph B. Simons.

6. Thomas Caplow, *Sociology of Work* (Minneapolis: University of Minnesota Press, 1954), p. 228.

7. Kenneth Kenniston, *The Young Radicals* (New York: Harcourt, Brace and World, Inc., 1968), pp. 284-290.

8. *Deuteronomy* 30:19.

Bibliography

Angel, Juvenal. *Occupations for Men and Women After 45.* 3rd ed. New York: World Trade Academy Press, 1964.

Baer, Max, and Roehr, Edward. *Occupational Information.* 3rd ed. Chicago: Science Research Associates, 1964.

Bell, Hugh M. "Ego-Involvement in Vocational Decisions." *Personnel and Guidance Journal* (July, 1960) : 732-735.

Bohn, Martin J. "Psychological Needs Related to Vocational Personality Types." *Journal of Counseling Psychology* (January, 1966) : 307-308.

Borow, Henry, ed. *Man in a World at Work.* Boston: Houghton-Mifflin Co., 1964.

Boyer, Gay. "Over 30 Despair: The Reality Gap." *Careers Today* (February, 1969) : 68-70, 94-95.

_____. "College (Dis)Placement Offices." *Careers Today* (March, 1969) : 82-84.

Boyer, William, and Walsh, Paul. "Are Children Born Unequal?" *Saturday Review* (October 19, 1968) : 61-63, 75-79.

Broom, H. N., and Longenecker, J. S. *Small Business Management.* Chicago: Southwestern Publishing Co., 1966.

Bruner, Jerome, "The New Educational Technology." In *Revolution in Teaching,* edited by Alfred D. Grazia. New York: Bantam Books, 1964.

California State Department of Education. *Apprenticeship Handbook for Education.* Sacramento, 1964.

_____. *Careers in California State Government.* Sacramento, 1969.

_____. *Counselors' Guide to College Majors.* Sacramento, 1966.

Caplow, Theodore. *The Sociology of Work.* Minneapolis: University of Minnesota Press, 1954.

Ciardi, John. "Manner of Speaking." *Saturday Review* (November 16, 1968) : 20-22.

College Placement Council, Inc. *College Placement Annual.* Bethlehem, Pa.: 1968, 1969, 1970.

Davis, James A. *Undergraduate Career Decisions.* Chicago: Aldine Publishing Co., 1965.

D'Costa, Ayres, and Wenefordner, David W. "The Cubistic Model of Vocational Interests." Paper presented at the American Educational Research Association Convention. Chicago, 1968.

Dictionary of Occupational Titles. 3rd ed. Volumes I, II, and Supplement. Washington, D.C.: U. S. Government Printing Office, 1965.

Dodgson, Charles. *The Complete Works of Lewis Carroll.* New York: Modern Library, Random House, n.d.

Erickson, Erik. *Childhood and Society.* 2nd ed. New York: W. W. Norton & Co., 1963.

_____. *Identity, Youth and Crisis.* New York: W. W. Norton & Co., 1968.

Eskow, Seymour. *Barron's Guide to the Two Year Colleges.* Woodbury, N.Y.: Barron's Educational Series, 1967.

Fromm, Erich. *The Sane Society.* New York: Holt, Rinehart & Winston, 1955.

Gleazer, Edmund, J., Jr. *This is the Community College.* Boston: Houghton-Mifflin Co., 1968.

Goodman, Paul. *Growing Up Absurd.* New York: Random House, 1960.

Hall, Mary Harrington. "A Convention with Peter Drucker." *Psychology Today* (March, 1968): 21-25, 70-72.

Hoffman, Bannech. *Tyranny of Testing.* New York: Collier Books ed., 1964.

Hoppock, Robert. *Occupational Information.* 3rd ed. New York: McGraw-Hill Book Co., 1967.

Horizons Unlimited. Chicago: American Medical Association, 1966.

Kaplan, Max. *Leisure in America.* New York: John Wiley & Sons, 1960.

Keniston, Kenneth. *The Uncommitted.* New York: Dell Publishing Co., 1965.

_____. *Young Radicals: Notes on Committed Youth.* New York: Harcourt, Brace & World, 1966.

Leonard, George B. *Education and Ecstasy.* New York: Delacorte Press, 1968.

Lovejoy, Clarence E. *Lovejoy's College Guide.* New York: Simon & Schuster, 1968.

Macdonald, William. "Graduates Fiddle While City Hall Burns." *Careers Today* (January, 1969): 38-40.

Manual for Strong Vocational Interest Blank. Stanford, Calif.: Stanford University Press, 1966.

Murphy, Franklin D. "The Time-Honored Student Restlessness." *Intercollegian,* orientation issue (1967): 10-13.

Nosow, Sigmund, and Form, William, eds. *Man, Work and Society.* New York: Basic Books, 1962.

Occupational Outlook Handbook. Washington, D.C.: U.S. Government Printing Office, 1966-67 ed.

Osipow, Samuel. *Theories of Career Development.* New York: Appleton-Century-Crofts, 1968.

Peters, Herman J., and Hansen, James C., eds. *Vocational Guidance and Career Development.* New York: The Macmillan Co., 1966.

Piel, Gerald. Address before the 1964 Conference of the Association for Higher Education.

Pitt, Gavin, and Smith, R. W. *The Twenty-Minute Lifetime: A Guide to Career Planning.* Englewood Cliffs, N.J.: Prentice-Hall, 1959.

Reeves, Vernon H. *Your College Degree*. Chicago: Science Research Associates, 1968.

Riesman, Frank, and Gartner, Alan. "New Careers and Pupil Learning." *California Teachers Association Journal* (March, 1969): 6-9.

Roe, Anne. *The Psychology of Occupations*. New York: John Wiley & Sons, 1956.

Rood, Allan. *Job Strategy*. New York: McGraw-Hill Book Co., 1961.

Rosenthal, Robert, and Jacobsen, Lenore. *Pygmalion in the Classroom*. New York: Holt, Rinehart & Winston, 1968.

Roth, Robert; Hershenson, David B.; and Hilliard, Thomas; eds. *The Psychology of Vocational Development*. Boston: Allyn & Bacon, 1970.

Sandman, Peter M. *Unabashed Career Guide*. New York: The Macmillan Co., 1969.

Schein, Edgar H. "The First Job Dilemma." *Psychology Today* (March, 1968): 26-37.

Silberman, Charles E. *The Myths of Automation*. New York: Harper & Row, Publishers, 1966.

Silva, Michael. "Big Government Wants You." *Careers Today* (January, 1969): 34-37, 75.

Steinberg, Leonard J. *Guide to Careers Through College Majors*. San Diego: Robert R. Knapp Publisher, 1966.

Strong, Edward. *Vocational Interest 18 Years After College*. Minneapolis: University of Minnesota Press, 1955.

Super, Donald E. *The Psychology of Careers*. New York: Harper & Bros., 1957.

Tebbel, John. "People and Jobs." *Saturday Review* (December 20, 1967): 8-12, 42.

Technical Education. Report of the Commission on Science Education. Washington, D.C.: American Association for the Advancement of Science Publication, 1968.

Twenty-five Technical Careers You Can Learn in Two Years or Less. Department of Health, Education, and Welfare. Washington, D.C.: U. S. Government Printing Office, 1971.

Vocational Guidance Quarterly "Johnny, the Band Leader" (1964): 194-196.

Wernick, Walter. *Career Education and the Elementary Teacher*. Worthington, Ohio: Charles A. Jones Publishing, 1972.

Wirtz, Willard W. *Labor and the Public Interest*. New York: Harper & Row, Publishers, 1964.

Wolfbein, Seymour. *Occupational Information*. New York: Random House, 1968.

Index

professions, 152-154; of skilled workers, 159; in small businesses, 146; in state and local governments, 150-152; as teacher aides, 160; in teaching, 160-161; as teaching assistants, 160; as technicians, 154-159

Eriksen, Erik, 49, 192

Ethical standards, 55

Experience as teacher, 75-80

Exploration of college courses, 75-77

Exploring a vocational choice, 109-120; in *Dictionary of Occupational Titles (DOT)*, 110-111; by interviews, 115-116; through library research, 109-112; in *Occupational Outlook Handbook,* 110; organizing the data, 116-120; in periodicals, 112-113; by visitations, 114-115

"Fantasy" jobs, 190, 192

Faulkner, William, 175-176

Fearing, Kenneth, 105-106

Federal departments and agencies, 148-150

Federal Service Entrance Examination, 150

Financial aids, 127-128

Finn, James, 161

Fromm, Erich, 15

General Aptitude Test Battery (GATB), 70-71

Gleazer, Edmund, Jr., 129, 138-139

Goals, career, 193

Goodman, Paul, 58-59

Government service, 148-152

Great Stone Face (Hawthorne), 193-194

Gregg, Elizabeth, 13

Guide to Careers Through College Majors (Steinberg), 112

Guide to Sources of Information on Scholarships, 128

Hamlet, 16

Havighurst, Robert, 16, 24-25, 191

Hawthorne, Nathaniel, 193-194

Hodgsen, James D., 187-188

Hoppock, Robert, 168

Hoffman, Banesh, 72

Holand, John L., 84, 100

Huizinga, Johan, 13-14, 19

Identity crises, 49, 50

Industrial needs. *See* Trends in industrial needs

Industries: goods-producing, 32, 33, 35; service-producing, 33, 35

Information, occupational, 30-41. *See also* Exploring a vocational choice

Information, vocational, 109-120. *See also* Exploring a vocational choice

Initial work stage, 166, 167

Interest tests: definition of, 65; interpretation of, 65-69; Kuder Preference Record, 67; Strong Vocational Interest Blank, 66; utilizing, 67, 68

Interpretation of interest tests, 65-69

Interests versus aptitudes, 68, 69

Interviews of workers, 115, 116

"Interviews with Electronic Workers," 118-120

IQ tests, 63, 64

Job characteristics, 23-24

Job involvement in "data," "people," and "things," 87-89

Job ratings, 23-24

Job satisfaction, studies in, 26-27

Jobs, part-time, 78-79

Jung, Carl, 9

Junior college. *See* Community college

Kenniston, Kenneth, 191, 193

Kuder Preference Record, 67

Leonard, George, 161

Library research, 109-113

Life style, 1, 82-84

Lovejoy's *Career and Vocational School Guide,* 125

Lovejoy's *College Guide,* 137

Lovejoy's *Scholarship Guide,* 128

MacLeish, Achibald, 41

Macmillan Job Guide to American Corporations, 144

Macy, John W. Jr., 149

Majors, college. *See* College majors

Manufacturing company organization, 145

Mature worker, 191, 192

Military service career opportunities, 125

Miller, August, 15

"Miniver Cheevy" (Robinson), 103-104

Minnesota Paper Board Form, 70

Moral standards, 55

Motivation and achievement, 94

Motivation and work choice, 91, 94

Myths of Automation (Silberman), 38

Nader, Ralph, 172-173

National Defense Education Act (NDEA), 127

Occupational education, 124-139. *See also* Vocational education and training

Occupational Outlook Handbook, 110

Older worker, 178-183; employment counseling, 180; placement, 179-180; productivity 178-179; training, 182-183

On-the-job experience, 77-80

Organization of manufacturing company, 145

Osipow, Samuel, 94